THE DEMAND FOR CANADIAN IMPORTS

T0326903

CANADIAN STUDIES IN ECONOMICS

A series of studies, edited by Wm. C. Hood, sponsored by the Canadian Social Science Research Council, and published with financial assistance from the Canada Council.

THE DEMAND

FOR CANADIAN

IMPORTS

1926-55

BY

Murray C. Kemp

UNIVERSITY OF TORONTO PRESS: 1962

Reprinted 2017
ISBN 978-1-4875-9222-6 (paper)

To V. M. K.

PREFACE

THE PROBLEMS DISCUSSED in this book have occupied me intermittently since the autumn of 1956. During that period I have become heavily indebted to several institutions and to many individuals. My initial sponsor was the Nuffield Foundation, which awarded me a travelling fellowship for the year 1956–57. Since then I have spent two summers as the guest of the Institute for Economic Research at Queen's University, Kingston, Ontario. Computations have been subsidized by the Institute for Economic Research at Queen's University, the Committee on Research at McGill University, and the Ford Foundation Faculty Research Fund at the Massachusetts Institute of Technology. The Economic Research Corporation of Montreal has made available its computing and duplicating facilities, as well as the technical advice of its personnel. I am deeply appreciative of the assistance extended to me by each of these institutions. Professor David W. Slater, a pioneer in the analysis of Canadian imports, provided me with expert advice on innumerable occasions. Mrs. Doris Bradley, of the *Economist*, supplied me with indices of tramp shipping freight rates back to 1926. Mr. Eric Sievwright, then with the Shell Oil Company of Canada, provided me with technical information concerning the importation of petroleum. Mr. L. A. Shackleton, Chief of the External Trade Section, Dominion Bureau of Statistics, provided me with the f.o.b. import price series. I have benefited greatly from the comments on earlier drafts of individual chapters by Merritt Brown, Peter Cornell, Stephen Kaliski, Edwin Kuh, David Slater, Robert Thompson, and Jacques Parizeau. Finally, I have had two singularly intelligent and uncomplaining assistants, Peter M. Mieszkowski and Terry Gigantes, who have borne the brunt of the computational work and saved me from many blunders. Comprehensive studies of the petroleum and petroleum products, coal and fuels categories may be found in "Canadian Import Demand for Fuels: A Study of Aggregation Bias in Econometric Research" (1959) by Peter M. Mieszkowski. A detailed analysis of the demand for imported automobiles may be found in "The Market for Automobiles in Canada: An Econometric Study" (1960) by Terry Gigantes. Both studies are unpublished M.A. theses deposited in the Redpath Library, McGill University, Montreal.

M. C. K.

CONTENTS

THE DEMAND FOR CANADIAN IMPORTS

CHAPTER ONE

INTRODUCTION

MY INITIAL OBJECTIVE in embarking on this study was a set of estimates of the principal parameters of Canadian import demand functions. It soon became evident, however, that estimation could not proceed on the basis of the then available aggregative time series of price and value and that new, less aggregative series would have to be pieced together from the trade returns. In reaching this conclusion, the following line of reasoning was decisive. Canada imports an unusually wide variety of commodities;[1] no single category dominates the rest. Aggregative price series, therefore, are averages of a similar variety of individual commodity prices. As Guy Orcutt has noted,

> . . . it seems reasonable to assume that historical price changes have been largest for those goods that admittedly have low price elasticities of demand. Thus we expect raw material and agricultural prices to show a wider range of price fluctuations than do products in general. This means that most of the price changes in the historical price indices of imports lumped together were due to price changes of commodities with inelastic demands. Since these price changes were associated with only small quantity adjustments, the estimated price elasticity of all imports might well be low. However, if as is usually assumed, the price elasticities of supply of exports are very high, at least in the long run, then it follows that a depreciation would result in sizable and more or less uniform price declines for imports of non-depreciating areas. The effect on quantity of imports or exports of a more or less uniform price change would evidently be substantially greater than in a situation in which most of the price changes were for products with inelastic demands or supplies.[2]

The assumption of high price elasticities of foreign export supply is, of course, crucial to this line of reasoning. Hence the argument cannot be applied indiscriminately. But for Canada, at least during the period under study, the assumption seems not inappropriate.[3]

The construction of the new series proved to be a gruelling and exceedingly time-consuming task. The initial objective was pushed into the background, and the writer should now regard the estimates of demand parameters as of distinctly secondary value in relation to the series themselves. We now have value and, in most cases, price and quantity series for seventeen fairly homogeneous categories of commodity imports for the peacetime years of the period 1926–55. The estimation of parameters, initially viewed as the core of the undertaking, has been merely a pleasant canter home after a day's hard riding in the sun. This imbalance of pleasure and pain is somewhat redressed, however, by the reflection that the new series may prove of value to other investigators.

Canadian imports are particularly suitable material for a study of this kind. First, and most important, the basic trade returns are among the most reliable compiled. Second, with only minor qualifications (to be noted in due course), the demand for Canadian imports has, throughout the period examined, been unfettered by quantitative commodity restrictions or exchange controls. Third, with the exception of military requirements (which are excluded from the scope of the study) direct governmental demand for imports has been negligible. Finally, the period has been free of substantial inflations or deflations, and hence of any substantial volume of speculative advance or decrease in buying. On the other hand, the relative prices for individual categories of imports have displayed roughly the same relative variability as income. The explanatory variables have displayed some degree of collinearity, but the coefficient of correlation between income and price has generally been less than 0.7 in absolute value. The conditions were not unfavourable, therefore, for obtaining statistically significant estimates of the price coefficients.

The plan of the book is straightforward. In chapter II and in appendixes II and III the major problems of data assembly, and the *ad hoc* solutions adopted, are described. In chapter III and in appendixes IV and V certain problems of statistical method are discussed. In particular, the technique of least squares regression is defended. The detailed results of the regression analysis are set out in chapter IV, with brief commentaries.

"DBS" will be used throughout as an abbreviation for the Dominion Bureau of Statistics, the principal data-collecting and data-publishing agency in Canada.

In general, equations are labelled with a pair of numbers, the first of which indicates the chapter or appendix in which the equation first appears. Thus the fifth equation in chapter III is labelled (3.5), the first equation in appendix IV is labelled (IV.1). Tables are labelled in a similar fashion.

CHAPTER TWO

THE STATISTICAL DATA

THE BASIC SOURCE of information on Canadian imports is *Trade of Canada*, which is published annually by DBS and which contains, for individual commodities, f.o.b. values (at point of consignment), duty collected, and, where a unit of quantity is available, physical quantities. In addition to this detail, *Trade of Canada* contains aggregative value series based on four separate principles of commodity classification. Additional aggregative series, based on two distinct principles of classification, are published quarterly by the Bank of Canada in its monthly *Statistical Summary*. Finally, David W. Slater, in a study prepared for the Royal Commission on Canada's Economic Prospects,[1] has developed series based on two further classifications.

There exists, therefore, a considerable variety of alternative classificatory schemes from which to choose. For present purposes, the most satisfactory principles of classification are (a) homogeneity of price movements and (b) homogeneity of income and price elasticities. But there is available insufficient evidence concerning individual price movements or individual price and income elasticities to make practicable reliance on either principle. Resort has been had, therefore, to the proxy criterion of homogeneity in end use. Of all the available classificatory schemes, Slater's "functional classification" comes closest to satisfying the requirement of homogeneity in end use and is employed throughout the present study.[2] The seventeen "functional classes" defined by Slater are: food and food materials; beverages and tobacco; clothing and textiles, personal furnishings, and materials for such uses; furniture, household appliances, radio and television; miscellaneous consumer durables; miscellaneous consumer perishables; automobiles, trucks, and parts; machinery and equipment (excluding automobiles, trucks and parts, aircraft and parts); aircraft and parts; materials for investment in structures; miscellaneous investment goods; coal; petroleum and petroleum products; fuels; basic chemicals; unassigned industrial materials; and special items. It proved to be impossible to obtain reliable f.o.b. price indices for the aircraft and parts, miscellaneous investment goods, basic chemicals, and special items categories. For these four categories, therefore, quantity series (value series divided by f.o.b. price series) could not be obtained, and the estimation of demand parameters has not been attempted. (However, the value and duty series are set out in appendix I.) Nor could separate f.o.b. price indices for the two classes of consumer goods be constructed. However, an index for the combined consumer goods category was available. Thus, four of Slater's seventeen categories had to be ignored and two of the remaining categories have been amalgamated, leaving twelve to be examined. For most of these, the captions are sufficiently descriptive.[3] Only the catch-all, unassigned industrial materials, needs special comment. Its main components are basic iron and steel products which do not fall naturally into one of the other categories, iron ore, rubber, and general purpose non-ferrous and non-metallic mineral products.[4]

The investigation was handicapped at the outset by serious gaps in the statistical data. In the first place, Slater's figures are of current values and cover only selected years from 1928 to 1955. In the second place, f.o.b. price indices, essential for deflating the value series, were available for selected years only. Finally, indices of import prices at the Canadian wholesale or retail level, essential in any investigation of the effect of price on demand, were unavailable. The first gap could be filled by anyone willing to spend several tedious weeks with *Trade of Canada* and a desk computer. Value series have been constructed for sixteen categories and for total commodity imports. With the exception of the war years 1940–45, they extend from 1926 to 1955. The second gap was filled, at my request, by DBS. The f.o.b. price series will be described in detail below. The third gap was more difficult to span. A bridge has been constructed, but in spots the foundations are not as secure as one would like. There are two possible approaches to the problem, and both have been tried. The first consists in taking the published DBS wholesale or retail price relatives of those commodities which are mainly imported, or which are tolerably homogeneous with imports, and in applying weights proportional to import values in selected years. But for only five of the twelve categories—food and food materials, materials for investment in structures, coal, petroleum and petroleum products, and fuels[5]—was the available coverage sufficient to justify this approach. Series constructed by this method will be called *direct* price series. The second method is more roundabout. It consists in adjusting the f.o.b. indices for estimates of freight and insurance, tariffs, excise taxes, wholesalers' mark-ups, and, where the relevant price index is a retail price index, for sales taxes and retailers' mark-ups. Series constructed in this way will be called indirect price series. The second method was available for all categories except petroleum and petroleum products and fuels.[6] For three categories, therefore, two independent price series are available. They provide the basis for alternative estimates of the price (and income) elasticities of demand for those categories. It was impossible to construct an index of transportation costs for 1946, hence the indirect price index could not be computed for that year. But since controls over wages, prices, and (finally) rent were removed only in 1946, the loss of that year is immaterial.

PRICE SERIES

Since the price series are published here for the first time, a detailed account of their construction and coverage is called for.

The F.O.B. Price Indices

These are of the Laspeyres type, with weights proportional to the 1935–39 f.o.b. values. It is difficult to estimate the coverage with precision because, as will be explained presently, the individual price series do not in every case correspond exactly to the commodity descriptions of the trade returns. Further, the coverage varies from year to year, for some categories quite sharply. In most instances the variations in coverage reflect changes in the relative composition of a category—a particularly good example is the sharp postwar increase in importance, within the category materials for investment in structures, of steel pipes. In a few instances, however, there occurred a change in the composition of the basket of goods defining the price index; the coverage of the food

TABLE 2.1
COVERAGE OF F.O.B. AND INDIRECT PRICE INDICES

$$\left(100 \; \frac{\text{value of imports represented in the index}}{\text{value of imports}}\right)$$

	Per Cent			
Category	1928	1938	1954	Average
Food and food materials	9	12	48	33
Beverages and tobacco	41	41	43	42
Clothing and textiles, etc.	32	49	51	45
Furniture, household appliances, etc.	84	77	71	77
Miscellaneous consumer goods	43	47	42	43
Automobiles, trucks, and parts	97	97	97	97
Materials for investment in structures	21	31	32	30
Coal	88	96	95	93
Petroleum and petroleum products	85	91	69	74
Fuels	86	92	77	80
Unassigned industrial materials	27	26	27	27

and food materials index, for example, increased sharply after the war. Accordingly, in Table 2.1 are set out estimates of the coverage of the price series for each of three years—one pre-Ottawa Agreements year, one post-Ottawa year, and one postwar year—as well as a value-weighted average of the coverages of the three years.

In general, the indices are based on individual unit values. There are, however, important exceptions to this rule: when no standardized and stable quantity unit exists, "comparable" United States wholesale prices or, occasionally, Canadian wholesale prices are used. Each of these three types of price is, of course, only a more or less good estimate of the price actually paid. There is no justification for relying heavily on Canadian prices for they differ from the prices actually paid by freight, a highly volatile element, and by Canadian import duty and excise taxes, less volatile but nevertheless capable of substantial year-to-year variation. Fortunately, in the present case no index draws heavily on Canadian price quotations; in the case of only one category, food and food materials, do Canadian prices represent as much as 10 per cent of the coverage. United States wholesale prices, however, have been used more extensively; the price series for some categories, indeed, are based almost entirely on United States prices. This does not, however, rule out the possibility of deriving tolerably accurate estimates from the series. For the categories involved—furniture, household appliances, etc.; machinery and equipment; consumer goods; automobiles, trucks, and parts; materials for investment in structures—are precisely those of which the United States is the overwhelmingly dominant supplier. United States wholesale prices include, of course, local sales and excise taxes, most of which would be evaded by exports; but these taxes are a sufficiently small and stable part of price to be ignored.

There are, of course, innumerable reasons for expecting unit values to differ from the true f.o.b. prices paid. Even at the level of detail of the trade returns, there is some measure of aggregation, however trivial. Further, unit values are based on *values for duty*. To the extent that the latter in turn are based on invoice values, and to the extent that invoice values are understated, a downward bias is imparted to the unit values, considered as estimates of the true f.o.b. prices. Again, during certain periods and in the case of specific commodities, the application of the dumping provisions has resulted in possibly substantial discrepancies between the amounts actually paid and the values for duty. It does not appear, however, that these difficulties constitute sufficient grounds for refusing to use the f.o.b. series. To justify such a refusal not only would it be necessary to show that there exists substantial aggregation bias in the individual unit values, or that there is substantial invoice cheating, or that the "dumping" valuations are much in excess of the amounts actually paid; it would be necessary to show further that the bias, or cheating, or excess valuation fluctuated appreciably from year to year. There is, however, a more serious objection to the use of unit values. Value for duty is based on the official exchange rates on the day the goods pass the customs. Normally the official rates vary from day to day

TABLE 2.2

TYPE OF PRICE QUOTATION USED IN CONSTRUCTION OF F.O.B. PRICE INDICES

Category of Imports	Type of Price Quotation
Food and food materials	Mainly unit values, about 10 per cent Canadian wholesale prices
Beverages and tobacco	Unit values
Textiles, clothing, etc.	Mainly unit values, about 15 per cent United States wholesale prices
Furniture, household appliances, etc.	Mainly United States wholesale prices, a small proportion United States retail prices
Miscellaneous consumer goods	Mainly United States wholesale prices
Automobiles, trucks, and parts	United States wholesale prices
Machinery and equipment	United States wholesale prices
Materials for investments in structures	Mainly United States wholesale prices
Coal	Unit values
Petroleum and petroleum products	Unit values
Fuels	Unit values
Industrial materials	Mainly unit values, about 15 per cent United States wholesale prices

and accurately reflect variations in the market rates. However, there have been lengthy periods when, in the case of particular currencies, the official rates have diverged substantially from the corresponding market rates. Imports billed in those currencies have, accordingly, been substantially overvalued or undervalued. The most notorious instance was the failure, over a period of more than two years, of the official rates to reflect the depreciation of sterling[7] (and certain other currencies[8]) in the early 'thirties. There resulted a substantial overvaluation for customs purposes of the British content of imports paid for in sterling. Jacques Parizeau has constructed price indices from which the distortion introduced by arbitrary official rates of exchange has been as far as possible removed. Unfortunately, Parizeau's indices are aggregative f.o.b. indices and therefore are unsuited to our purpose.[9]

The Direct Price Series

These were constructed from the published DBS wholesale price relatives of those commodities which are mainly imported or are close substitutes for imported commodities. The weights are proportional to the average values of the corresponding imports in the years 1928, 1938, and 1954. For the petroleum and petroleum products and coal categories, the indices were lifted, almost bodily, from the DBS index of wholesale prices.[10] The index for fuels was constructed by combining those for coal and petroleum and petroleum products, with weights of 0.32 and 0.68 respectively. As already noted, the method was feasible for only five categories. The coverage of the indices is set out in Table 2.3.

TABLE 2.3

COVERAGE OF DIRECT PRICE INDICES

$$\left(100 \ \frac{\text{value of imports represented in index}}{\text{value of imports}}\right)$$

	Per Cent			
Category	1928	1938	1954	Average
Food and food materials	52	60	61	58
Materials for investment in structures	20	23	40	35
Coal	80	95	93	89
Petroleum and petroleum products	78	95	85	86
Fuels	79	95	87	86

The "Indirect" Price Series

These were obtained from the f.o.b. series by correcting for insurance and freight charges, import duties, excise duties, wholesalers' mark-ups and, where it was appropriate, for sales taxes and retailers' mark-ups. Information on mark-ups is not available; *faute de mieux*, it has been assumed that they are a constant proportion of the landed value. Similarly, the available information on insurance rates is sketchy and inadequate. It seemed reasonable, however, to assume that insurance charges have been a small and stable proportion of landed value; accordingly, they too have been ignored. But the more volatile elements of price—transport costs, import duties, and sales and excise taxes—cannot be passed over so lightly. The method by which correction was made for these factors is described in appendix III.

An indirect price index for aggregate imports was constructed by taking a weighted average of the indices for individual categories.[11] The weights were

TABLE 2.4

WEIGHTS USED IN AGGREGATE IMPORT PRICE INDEX

Category	Per Cent
Consumers' goods	
Food and food materials	15.04
Beverages and tobacco	1.24
Clothing and textiles, etc.	14.63
Furniture, household appliances, etc.	2.93
Automobiles, trucks, and parts	7.69
Miscellaneous consumers' goods	8.68
All consumers' goods	50.21
Producers' goods	
Machinery and equipment	21.18
Materials for investment in structures	5.63
Unassigned industrial materials	12.97
Fuels	10.01
All producers' goods	49.79

proportional to the average of the f.o.b. values for the three years 1928, 1938, and 1954 and are set out in Table 2.4. Where an indirect price index was available, it was used; otherwise, as in the case of petroleum and petroleum products, the direct price index was used. It should be noted that the aggregate import price index covers only those categories for which direct or indirect price indices exist. In particular, the index does not cover the categories aircraft and parts, miscellaneous investment goods, basic chemicals, and special items.

CHAPTER THREE

THE METHOD OF ESTIMATION

MOST OF THE ESTIMATES of price and income elasticities set out in this chapter were obtained by least squares linear regression of quantity on real income (or output) and on one or two price variables, including an index of the price of imports. All price variables were deflated by a general index either of wholesale or of retail prices. Both the method of deflation and the decision to employ the familiar but *démodé* technique of least squares call for justification. The present chapter contains a detailed, perhaps overdrawn, defence of the method of least squares in the present special context. A few difficulties peculiar to the material and period studied are discussed. And, finally, some implications of the method of deflation are noted.

The method of estimation must, of course, be suited to the stochastic model which, it is supposed, has generated the sample data. In this connection it has been argued, by Orcutt[1] and others, that least squares regression is an inappropriate method for estimating import demand parameters; that, in particular, it is very likely to yield estimates which are biased towards zero. It is necessary at the outset, therefore, to provide some sort of defence of the method.[2] It will be argued that, for most categories of imports, certain sufficient conditions for unbiasedness hold to a satisfactory approximation. Note that only the approximate satisfaction of the conditions is claimed. It would be foolish for any econometrician working with annual time series to claim that his technique of estimation is ideally suited to the task. Further to this general disclaimer of too-serious intent, the category automobiles, trucks, and parts is specifically exempted from the defence offered. For reasons which will be given later, that category seems to be peculiarly ill-suited to the method of least squares. An attempt has been made, without much success, to estimate the coefficients of demand for automobiles by means of the method of limited information maximum likelihood.[3] For details of the statistical model used, the reader is referred to chapter IV.

THE RELEVANCE OF LEAST SQUARES

As is well known, least squares estimates are unbiased only if the error or disturbance variable is statistically independent of the regressors. At least two reasons have been advanced for believing that, in the case of import demand functions, this condition may not be satisfied. In the first place, it may be impossible for the quantity variable fully to absorb all variations of the error variable because the quantity and price variables, say, must satisfy not only a demand relation but also a supply relation.[4] In the second place, the error variable may be comprised in part of errors in the measurement of one or more of the regressors and hence be correlated with the measured regressors.[5] These two possibilities are considered in turn.

Multiple Relations

Consider the following linearized version of our import demand function:

(3.1) $$X = \alpha_0 + \alpha_1 P + \alpha_2 P_1 + \alpha_3 Y_1 + \epsilon_1$$

In (3.1) X is the demand for Canadian imports of a particular class, P is the price, in terms of Canadian dollars, of imports of that class, P_1 is some general Canadian price index (wholesale or retail depending on the category of imports), and Y_1 is the output or real disposable personal income of Canada, the choice of definition depending again on the category of imports. ϵ_1 is an unobserved error variable with an expectation of zero, and α_0, α_1, α_2, and α_3 are constants. Now each of the import quantities is quite small in relation to Y_1 and in relation to the quantity counterpart of P_1. It is, therefore, not unreasonable to assume that ϵ_1 is statistically independent of P_1 and Y_1, that is, that fluctuations in the demand for a particular category of imports have a negligible effect on the general price level and on the level of income or output. In other words, P_1 and Y_1 can be treated as predetermined variables, suitable grist for the least squares mill. The question to be explored is whether, knowing that a supply relation lurks in the background, it is reasonable to assume that ϵ_1 is also statistically independent of P, the price (in Canadian dollars) of Canadian imports of a particular class. The answer will be seen to depend on the assumptions made about the mathematical form, and the pattern of shifts, of the supply relation. In the following discussion it will be convenient to lump together all countries except Canada as "the rest of the world."

For many individual commodities and, in two or three instances, for whole categories of commodities, Canada is a major *foreign* buyer of its suppliers' wares. In the case of a few individual commodities Canada even buys a large part of its suppliers' total output. But, if attention is confined to the broad categories of imports recognized in this study, there is not a single instance in which Canada takes more than 10 per cent of its suppliers' total output. It follows that the Canadian import supply functions must be highly elastic.[6] Without serious error they may be assumed to be infinitely elastic. Then the supply or price-forming relations may be written in the general form

(3.2) $$\frac{P}{R} = \beta_0 + \beta_1 D_2 + \beta_2 P_2 + v_2$$

where D_2 is the demand of the rest of the world for this particular class of Canadian imports; P_2 is a general index of prices in the rest of the world; R is an index of the prices, in terms of Canadian dollars, of the currencies of other countries and therefore serves to convert P into the currencies of other countries; β_0, β_1, and β_2 are constants (β_0, β_2 positive); and v_2 is an unobserved error variable, with expectation zero and assumed to be independent of R and P_2. D_2 appears also in the foreign demand relation

$$D_2 = \gamma_0 + \gamma_1 \frac{P}{R} + \gamma_2 P_2 + \gamma_3 Y_2 + u_2$$

where Y_2 is the output or real disposable personal income (depending on the category of imports) of the rest of the world; γ_0, γ_1, γ_2, and γ_3 are constants;

and u_2 is an unobserved error variable with expectation zero and assumed to be independent of R, P_2, and Y_2. Substituting for D_2 in (3.2),

$$(3.3) \quad \frac{P}{R} = \frac{\beta_0 + \beta_1\gamma_0}{1 - \beta_1\gamma_1} + \frac{\beta_1\gamma_2 + \beta_2}{1 - \beta_1\gamma_1} P_2 + \frac{\beta_1\gamma_3}{1 - \beta_1\gamma_1} Y_2 + \frac{\beta_1 u_2 + v_2}{1 - \beta_1\gamma_1}.$$

In the remaining developments it will not be necessary to distinguish the predetermined variables, P_2 and Y_2. Accordingly a new variable

$$Z = P_2 + \frac{\beta_1\gamma_3}{\beta_1\gamma_2 + \beta_2} Y_2$$

is defined and (3.3) is written as

$$\frac{P}{R} = \frac{\beta_0 + \beta_1\gamma_0}{1 - \beta_1\gamma_1} + \frac{\beta_1\gamma_2 + \beta_2}{1 - \beta_1\gamma_1} Z + \frac{\beta_1 u_2 + v_2}{1 - \beta_1\gamma_1}$$

or, more simply, as

$$(3.4) \quad \frac{P}{R} = \mu_0 + \mu_1 Z + \epsilon_2$$

where μ_0 and μ_1 are the constants

$$\mu_0 = \frac{\beta_0 + \beta_1\gamma_0}{1 - \beta_1\gamma_1}$$

$$\mu_1 = \frac{\beta_1\gamma_2 + \beta_2}{1 - \beta_1\gamma_1}$$

and

$$(3.5) \quad \epsilon_2 = \frac{\beta_1 u_2 + v_2}{1 - \beta_1\gamma_1}$$

(ϵ_2 is, of course, statistically independent of Z). Expressing the value of each variable as its expectation plus a deviation from its expectation, (3.4) may be rewritten as

$$(3.6) \quad p + E(P) = \mu_0[r + E(R)] + \mu_1[z + E(Z)][r + E(R)] + \epsilon_2[r + E(R)]$$

where E is the instruction to take the expectation and lower-case letters stand for deviations. Taking the expectation of both sides of (3.6)

$$(3.7) \quad E(P) = \mu_0 E(R) + \mu_1[E(R)E(Z) + E(rz)].$$

Subtracting (3.7) from (3.6),

$$(3.8) \quad p = [\mu_0 + \mu_1 E(Z)]r + \mu_1[E(R)z + rz - E(rz)] + \epsilon_2 E(R) + \epsilon_2 r.$$

It is now possible, at last, to set out the conditions under which p and ϵ_1 (see equation (3.1)) are independent. Multiplying (3.8) by ϵ_1, and taking the expectation of both sides of the product,

$$E(p\epsilon_1) = \mu_1 E(rz\epsilon_1) + E(R)E(\epsilon_1\epsilon_2) + E(\epsilon_1\epsilon_2 r).$$

If, as we may suppose, ϵ_1, ϵ_2, r and z are symmetrically distributed, $E(rz\epsilon_1)$ and $E(\epsilon_1\epsilon_2 r)$ vanish.[7] Hence,

$$E(p\epsilon_1) = E(R)E(\epsilon_1\epsilon_2).$$

Thus a sufficient condition for the independence of p and ϵ_1 is that ϵ_1 and ϵ_2 be independent, that is, that shifts of the import function should be independent of shifts of the import supply function. It will now be suggested that, for Canada, this is a reasonable assumption.

As a first step, recall that the import demand function is an excess demand function and that ϵ_1 is the difference between the error variable of the aggregate demand function (for imports plus home-produced substitutes) of the importing country, say u_1, and the error variable of the domestic supply function, say v_1. Thus

(3.9) $$\epsilon_1 = u_1 - v_1.$$

From (3.5) and (3.9), then,

$$E(\epsilon_1\epsilon_2) = \frac{\beta_1[E(u_1u_2) - E(u_2v_1)] + E(u_1v_2) - E(v_1v_2)}{1 - \beta_1\gamma_1}.$$

It seems reasonable to assume that $E(u_1v_2) = E(u_2v_1) = 0$, that is, that purely demand shifts in one country are independent of purely supply shifts in another. If this assumption is made,

$$E(\epsilon_1\epsilon_2) = \frac{\beta_1 E(u_1u_2) - E(v_1v_2)}{1 - \beta_1\gamma_1}.$$

Thus $E(\epsilon_1\epsilon_2) = 0$, and the least squares estimates of the α's are unbiased if

(3.10) $$\beta_1 E(u_1u_2) = E(v_1v_2).$$

Alternative sufficient conditions for (3.10) to hold are

(3.11) $$E(u_1u_2) = E(v_1v_2) = 0$$

and

(3.12) $$\beta_1 = E(v_1v_2) = 0.$$

The first of these sufficient conditions states that purely demand shifts for traded commodities are, among trading countries, independent of each other; and that purely supply shifts are also independent of each other. The second condition states that purely supply shifts are independent of each other and that the *aggregate* supply elasticities of imported commodities (not merely the *export* supply elasticities) are, in the supplying countries, infinite. It would be extravagant to pretend that, for any of the categories employed in the present study, (3.11) is satisfied, even to a close approximation. Canadian and United States consumers, for example, are subjected to similar types of advertising and their views stem from similar sources of information and opinion. Hence, it would be unrealistic to assume that $E(u_1u_2) = 0$. But condition (3.12) is another matter. In most manufacturing industries, and in some industries producing raw materials, approximately constant returns to scale prevail.[8] That is, $\beta_1 = 0$ (see equation (3.2)). Further, if v_1 and v_2 are not confounded with trend factors, it would seem reasonable to assume that supply shifts are independent of each other, that is, that $E(v_1v_2) = 0$. The category automobiles, trucks, and parts is an outstanding exception to this generalization and for that reason is handled by the method of limited information.

Errors of Observation

A case has been made for ignoring whatever bias may be introduced by the existence of more than one relation between the variables. There remains the possibility of bias arising from "errors of observation," particularly in the price variable.

If one of the regressors, say P, is subject to inaccurate measurement, least squares estimates will in general be biased estimates. This may be seen most easily in the simple two-variables case in which the import demand relation is written

$$X = \alpha P + \epsilon_1.$$

If the error with which P is measured is represented by ϵ the relation may be rewritten as

(3.13)
$$X = \alpha(P + \epsilon) + (\epsilon_1 - \alpha\epsilon).$$

It is evident that $(P + \epsilon)$ and $(\epsilon_1 - \alpha\epsilon)$ are, in general, not independent and that least squares applied to (3.13) will yield biased estimates of α.[9] More specifically, it can be shown that, unless the error ϵ is highly and negatively correlated with P, the bias will be "towards zero." It can be shown further that if more regressors are introduced, least squares estimates of their coefficients will, in general, be biased also—even though the additional regressors are measured without error.[10]

The "coverage" of the price series used in the present study varies from category to category and with the method by which they were constructed, but in no case is it complete. Further, primary price data may, as has been noted in chapter II, be inaccurately recorded or correspond only roughly to the *Trade of Canada* commodity descriptions. It is plain that errors are present. It is important, therefore, to arrive at some notion of the magnitude and direction of the bias and to distinguish those conclusions whose validity is independent of the bias from those which stand and fall with the magnitude of the bias.

There are two considerations which seem pertinent to this problem. The first suggests that in many cases the bias may be quite small. The other suggests that, at least in cases where the indirect price index is employed, the bias is likely to be not "towards zero" but "towards unity." In the first place, the coverage of many of the price series is almost complete. Tables 2.1 and 2.3 reveal, for example, that for the coal, petroleum and petroleum products, and fuels categories the coverage of the direct price series is at least 85 per cent. For the coal, petroleum and petroleum products, fuels, automobiles, trucks, and parts, and furniture, household appliances, etc. categories the coverage of the f.o.b. and indirect price series is at least 75 per cent.

In the second place, not only the price variable but also the dependent quantity variable is subject to an error of measurement. For each category the quantity series was obtained as the quotient of a value series and a price series.

In most regressions, the import price regressor is the *indirect* price index which, it will be recalled, is based on the f.o.b. price index. Thus fundamentally the same index is used as deflator and as regressor. Further, import values are recorded with a high degree of accuracy. It follows, therefore, that the error in the quantity index is highly and negatively correlated with the error in the price index. Discussion of the bias in this case is relegated to appendix IV. It is shown there that, for large samples and under the plausible assumption that the errors are independent of the true value of the price variables, the bias with which the price elasticities are estimated is not "towards zero" but "towards unity."

In a few regressions, however, the direct price index is used as a regressor, the f.o.b. index being retained as deflator. In this case, two different estimates of P are employed in the same regression, one as deflator and another as regressor. Each series is subject to error and, in the light of the methods by which the series was constructed, there is small reason to expect the errors to be correlated with each other. It follows that the error with which the quantity variable is measured no longer can be assumed to be correlated with the error in the price regressor. The problem of establishing the magnitude and sign of the bias in this case is taken up in appendix IV where it is shown that, if the error components of the two observed price variables are independent of each other and of the true values of the two prices, the bias will be towards zero.

It would seem, then, that all estimates will be biased, some towards zero but most of them towards unity. With the exception of those estimates based on low-coverage price indices the bias may be expected in either case to be small. But in all cases one should be prepared to apply some sort of informal correction to the estimates.

Finally, it should be noted that the coverages of the price indices differ only slightly as between the interwar and postwar periods (see Tables 2.1. and 2.3).[11] There is therefore no reason to expect the bias to differ substantially from one subperiod to the other. Hence conclusions concerning *changes* in the values of elasticities between the two periods are substantially independent of errors of measurement.

THE RELIABILITY OF THE ESTIMATES

It is customary in econometric work to calculate the standard errors of the estimates and the coefficient of multiple correlation, and to perform the familiar tests of significance based on the t- and F-distributions. Strictly, these tests are valid only when the specification of the relation the parameters of which are to be estimated is known *a priori*—that is, independently of the sample data. The standard errors of the estimates then describe the outcome of repeated sampling from a *given* probability model.

Economists, however, usually arrive at their specifications only after a good deal of experimentation with the sample data. Economic theory provides scant guidance in choosing the form of the relation and the list of regressors. Economists proceed by trial and error, examining alternative combinations of variables until a "satisfactory" relation is obtained. Typical criteria are accuracy of fit, the signs of the estimated coefficients, and the randomness of the residuals. The upshot is that the specification changes with the sample. It is no longer a question of repeated sampling from a succession of different models. Hence the usual tests of significance are of doubtful relevance. They are biased in favour of significance and, if blindly applied, will promote excessive confidence in the estimates.[12] Put otherwise, the sample data are employed not only to test hypotheses but also to select the hypotheses to be tested. The degrees of freedom remaining in the sample after the relation has been specified are fewer than is supposed in the usual tests of significance. So far no method has been devised of determining the *net* degrees of freedom.

This kind of experimentation can, of course, be defended. In particular, if the researcher has "spare" data which were not used in the derivation of the estimates and which therefore can be used to construct a forecasting test of his estimates, the usual tests of significance may well be abandoned. Since the writer is not in this happy position, however, the other extreme has been elected: in all cases, the list of regressors has been selected *a priori* and has been retained through thick and thin, whether or not particular estimates turn out to differ significantly from zero or to have the "wrong" sign.[13, 14]

Analysis of Residuals

As is well known, the usual tests of significance can be applied to the estimates of the price and income coefficients only if the error variable is independent of its time subscript, that is, free of autocorrelation. Durbin and Watson have developed a test of the significance of autocorrelation which is based on the calculated regression residuals.[15] Their test statistic "d" is calculated in all cases. Unfortunately, they were able to establish only upper and lower limits to the critical values of "d." Only when the calculated value of "d" is unambiguously significant, that is, when it falls short of the lower limit in the case of positive autocorrelation or exceeds the upper limit in the case of negative autocorrelation, will attention be drawn to its value. A 5 per cent level of significance will be used throughout.

A Specific Difficulty—Quantitative Restrictions

A special methodological difficulty was posed by the fact that, during certain years and with respect to certain commodities, quantitative import restrictions were imposed. The technique of control was not uniform—*ad hoc* legislation, certain administrative devices, and "gentlemen's agreements" with foreign powers all had their turn. Thus the exchange crisis of 1947 brought forth special legislation imposing quantitative restrictions retroactively to November of that year; the administration of the legislation relating to copyrights, health standards, and marking appears to have been considerably tightened during the depression years; and gentlemen's agreements have, at sundry times, limited imports of New Zealand cheddar cheese, Cuban sugar, and Japanese textiles. Of these examples only the first seems to have been sufficiently important to warrant special statistical procedures.

The restrictions were effective from November 17, 1947. They were designed to cut the value of imports by $300 million in 1948 and bore with particular severity on imports from the United States. They were of three main kinds.[16] The importation of certain foods (mainly fresh fruits, other than citrus fruits, and vegetables), tobacco, paper products, and electrical appliances was, with minor exceptions, prohibited. (Imports of these goods fell in value from $41 million in 1947 to $9 million in 1948.) Other commodities, notably textiles and citrus fruits, were put on quota. (Imports fell in value from $220 million in 1947 to $94 million in the following year.) Finally, an attempt was made, by licensing, to hold imports of capital goods, including automobiles, at roughly their 1947 value. (In fact the value of imports of these commodities within a year fell from $564 million to $519 million.) The more severe restrictions had been removed by the end of 1948 and nearly all important restrictions had been abolished by the end of the following year. There are, therefore, just two years, 1948 and 1949, that were substantially affected by the legislation. Further, of the twelve categories examined in this study only six were substantially restricted: food and food materials; furniture, household appliances, etc.; clothing and textiles, etc.; automobiles, trucks, and parts; miscellaneous consumer goods; and beverages and tobacco.

There are several ways in which the difficulty might have been handled, none of them quite satisfactory. Perhaps the simplest would have been to lump the years of restriction with the immediately succeeding years and to average. Under this procedure there would have been a considerable loss of information. The chief assumption on which the procedure is based is that importers *wait* for the relaxation of controls, that the excess demand for restricted imports does not spill into the markets for unrestricted goods (either home-produced goods or unrestricted imports). This assumption is, of course, a quite unreasonable one in the case of perishable goods, some of which were hardest hit by the restrictions; and, even in the case of durable commodities, it does not appear to be sufficiently realistic to warrant adoption. The method adopted was also quite simple: a dummy variable was introduced and given the values 1.0 for 1948, 0.5 for 1949, and zero for all others years.[17] The method is open to one major objection—it substantially begs the question of the relative severity of the restrictions in 1948 and 1949. The question is not entirely begged, for it is quite clear that the severity of the restrictions had been considerably *reduced* by the end of 1948, and that therefore the dummy variable should be assigned a lower value for 1949 than for 1948.[18]

WARTIME STRUCTURAL BREAKS

The second world war marked violent[19] shifts in many economic relationships. Accordingly, separate regressions have been run for the prewar and postwar periods and formal tests have been made of the hypothesis that no break occurred.[20] The same price and quantity series were used for the prewar and postwar regressions, though a case could be made for recomputing the series with weights appropriate to each of the subperiods. The difficulty with this procedure is that the formal tests of homogeneity would not then be strictly relevant. A brief description of the tests is contained in appendix v.

BIAS ARISING FROM THE METHOD OF PRICE DEFLATION

In all regressions the import price variable is deflated by a general wholesale or retail price index. Both deflators give representation to imported commodities; in particular, each of the twelve categories for which regressions are run is represented in each of the deflators. Thus the import price index appears in both the numerator and the denominator of the price ratio. It will be clear, I think, that this duplication will damp the variation of the price ratio and result in estimates of the price coefficient which are biased away from zero. However, the representation of individual import categories in the deflators is in every case very small and the bias may well be neglected.

CHAPTER FOUR

ESTIMATES OF THE PRICE AND INCOME ELASTICITIES OF IMPORT DEMAND

IN THE PRESENT CHAPTER the detailed results of the regression analyses are set out and examined. Part A contains the results, and an occasional brief note of explanation, interpretation, or emphasis related to individual categories. In Part B, I venture some more general comments on the estimates as a whole. The basic time series of quantities, prices, and incomes may be found in appendix I.

PART A: ESTIMATES

The following notation will be employed throughout the present chapter. Quantity and income units are defined in appendix I.

X = the volume of imports, that is, the value of imports in 1936 dollars.

X' = the volume of imports *per capita*.

X_h = the volume of home production, that is, the value of home production in 1936 dollars.

X_x = the volume of home production for export.

X^* = the number of automobiles imported.

X^*_h = the number of automobiles produced and sold at home.

X^*_x = the number of automobiles exported.

Y = disposable personal income.

Y' = disposable personal income *per capita*, deflated by the Consumer Price Index, 1936 = 10.

G = the gross national product in 1949 dollars.

P_d = the direct import price, deflated by the Consumer Price Index, 1936 = 10

P_i = the indirect import price, deflated by the Consumer Price Index, 1936 = 10.

P_h = the price of home-produced competing goods, deflated by the Consumer Price Index, 1936 = 10.

P_d' = the direct import price, deflated by the Wholesale Price Index, 1936 = 10.

P_i' = the indirect import price, deflated by the Wholesale Price Index, 1936 = 10.

P_h' = the price of home-produced competing goods, deflated by the Wholesale Price Index, 1936 = 10.

P_i'' = the indirect import price, undeflated, 1936 = 10.

P_h'' = the price of home-produced competing goods, undeflated, 1936 = 10.

P_c'' = the consumer price index, undeflated, 1936 = 10.

W = an index of wages in Canadian manufacturing industry, 1936 = 10.

t = time, $t_{1925} = 0$.

S = the number of automobiles registered on March 31.

V = a shift variable which assumes the value 1.0 in 1948, 0.5 in 1949, and 0.0 in all other years.

ω_i = the elasticity of demand for imports with respect to income or output.

η = the elasticity of demand for imports with respect to the price of imports.

η' = the (cross) elasticity of demand for imports with respect to the price of home-produced competing goods.

d = Durbin's and Watson's statistic.

$\bar{R}$ = the coefficient of multiple linear correlation, corrected for degrees of freedom.

$r(x, y)$ = the coefficient of simple linear correlation between x and y.

The estimated standard errors are given in brackets beneath the estimates of the coefficients. Asterisks indicate that the estimate does not differ significantly from zero. All tests of significance are conducted at the 5 per cent level. For the relevance of the F-statistic, see chapter III, section D, and appendix V.

Furniture, Household Appliances, Radio and Television

1926–39 $X' = 2.18 - 0.35P_i + 0.06\,Y'$ $\bar{R} = 0.87$
          (0.11)   (0.02)

   $d = 1.36$ $\eta = -4.10$ $\omega = 2.47$ $r(P_i,\ Y') = -0.48$

   Coverage of the price index: 80 per cent

1947–55 $X' = -19.74 - 0.01P_i + 0.41\,Y' - 1.23\,V$ $\bar{R} = 0.96$
             (0.18)   (0.07)   (0.42)

   $d = 1.65$ $\eta = -0.03$ $\omega = 7.65$

   Coverage of price index: 71 per cent

	Y'	V
P_i	-0.46	0.34
Y'		-0.51

1926–55 $X' = -0.97 - 0.23P_i + 0.12\,Y' - 2.00\,V$ $\bar{R} = 0.95$
             (0.13)   (0.01)   (0.46)

   $d = 1.06$ $\eta = -1.45$ $\omega = 3.10$

   Coverage of the price index: 73 per cent

	Y'	V
P_i	0.70	0.43
Y'		0.30

   $F(3, 16) = 12.81$: significant

In retrospect, the number of households might have been a more reasonable deflator than population. But it is doubtful whether the substitution of one deflator for the other would have changed the results appreciably.

Food and Food Materials (with Direct Price)

1926–39 $X' = -3.48 - 0.69P_d + 0.36P_h + 0.82\,Y'$ $\bar{R} = 0.91$
             (0.33)   (0.12)   (0.51)

   $d = 1.56$ $\eta = -0.67$ $\eta' = 0.36$ $\omega = 2.70$

   Coverage of price index: 56 per cent

	P_h	Y'
P_d	0.31	0.22
P_h		0.85

1947–55 $\quad X' = -3.63 + 0.39 P_d + 0.26 P_h - 0.47 Y' - 1.07 V \qquad \bar{R} = 0.94$
$\qquad\qquad\quad (0.16) \quad\ (0.06) \quad\ (0.29) \quad\ (0.31)$
$\qquad d = 3.23 \quad \eta = 0.50 \quad \eta' = 0.30 \quad \omega = -2.48$

Coverage of price index: 61 per cent

	P_h	Y'	V
P_d	0.11	-0.74	0.49
P_h		-0.32	0.32
Y'			-0.51

1926–55 $\quad X' = 1.36 - 0.70 P_d + 0.03 P_h + 1.41 Y' - 1.27 V \qquad \bar{R} = 0.71$
$\qquad\qquad\quad\ (0.28) \quad\ (0.06) \quad\ (0.46) \quad\ (1.20)$
$\qquad d = 1.17 \quad \eta = -0.77 \quad \eta' = 0.03 \quad \omega = 5.77$

Coverage of price index: 58 per cent

	P_h	Y'	V
P_d	0.85	0.90	0.46
P_h		0.92	0.36
Y'			0.30

$\qquad F(4, 14) = 9.01$: significant

Food and Food Materials (with Indirect Price)
1926–39 $\quad X' = -9.95 - 0.32 P_i + 0.32 P_h + 1.25 Y' \qquad \bar{R} = 0.89$
$\qquad\qquad\quad\ (0.28) \quad\ (0.14) \quad\ (0.81)$

$\qquad d = 1.16 \quad \eta = -0.34 \quad \eta' = 0.32 \quad \omega = 4.11$
Coverage of price index: 10 per cent

	P_h	Y'
P_i	0.80	0.57
P_h		0.85

1947–55 $\quad X' = 4.16 + 0.10 P_i + 0.22 P_h - 0.60 Y' - 0.72 V \qquad \bar{R} = 0.86$
$\qquad\qquad\quad (0.15) \quad\ (0.19) \quad\ (0.43) \quad\ (0.51)$
$\qquad d = 3.09 \quad \eta = 0.14 \quad \eta' = 0.25 \quad \omega = -3.17$

Coverage of price index: 48 per cent

	P_h	Y'	V
P_i	0.08	-0.74	0.10
P_h		-0.32	0.32
Y'			-0.51

1926–55 $\quad X' = -3.56 - 0.27 P_i - 0.06 P_h + 1.82 Y' - 2.56 V \qquad \bar{R} = 0.61$
$\qquad\qquad\quad\ (0.21) \quad\ (0.05) \quad\ (0.63) \quad\ (1.20)$
$\qquad d = 0.79 \quad \eta = -0.32 \quad \eta' = -0.06 \quad \omega = 7.44$

Coverage of price index: 33 per cent

	P_h	Y'	V
P_i	0.88	0.81	0.33
P_h		0.92	0.36
Y'			0.30

$$r(P_d, P_i) = 0.89$$

$F(4, 14) = 8.41$: significant
$r(P_d, P_i) = 0.58$ for 1926–39
$ = 0.68$ for 1947–55
$ = 0.89$ for 1926–55

The low coverage of the indirect price index, especially in the interwar period, is to be noted, as is the high sample correlation of income with direct price in the postwar period and with home price in the interwar period. The postwar residuals display significant negative autocorrelation.

Clothing and Textiles, Personal Furnishings, etc.

1926–39 $X' = -15.47 - 0.23P_i + 1.00P_h + 0.62Y'$ $\bar{R} = 0.78$
$ (1.37) \quad (2.81) \quad (0.37)$
$d = 0.71 \ \eta = -0.18 \ \eta' = 0.79 \ \omega = 1.62$
Coverage of indirect price index: 41 per cent

	P_h	Y'
P_i	0.85	0.68
P_h		0.21

1947–55 $X' = 46.37 + 0.81P_i - 2.04P_h - 0.32Y' - 1.22V$ $\bar{R} = 0.62$
$ (0.48) \quad (0.83) \quad (0.33) \quad (1.75)$
$d = 2.87 \ \eta = 0.91 \ \eta' = -2.06 \ \omega = -1.38$
Coverage of indirect price index: 51 per cent

	P_h	Y'	V
P_i	0.86	-0.56	0.06
P_h		-0.58	0.09
Y'			-0.51

1926–55 $X' = 19.67 + 1.35P_i - 2.39P_h + 0.09Y' - 0.00V$ $\bar{R} = 0.69$
$ (0.32) \quad (0.57) \quad (0.05) \quad (1.54)$
$d = 1.38 \ \eta = 1.25 \ \eta' = -2.10 \ \omega = 0.31$
Coverage of indirect price index: 45 per cent

	P_h	Y'	V
P_i	0.94	0.79	0.31
P_h		0.84	0.35
Y'			0.30

$F(4, 14) = 1.07$: not significant

The estimates are highly unreliable, partly because of the intercorrelation of the price variables and partly because of the low coverage of the direct and indirect price indices. Note also the significant autocorrelation displayed by the interwar residuals.

Beverages and Tobacco

1926–39 $X' = -4.84 + 0.14P_t + 0.13Y'$
             (0.04)   (0.02)
     $d = 2.07$ $\eta = 1.55$ $\omega = 3.84$
Coverage of price index: 41 per cent

$\bar{R} = 0.91$
$r(P_t, Y') = -0.26$

1947–55 $X' = 1.45 - 0.04P_t - 0.00Y' + 0.00V$
           (0.08)   (0.02)   (0.14)
     $d = 2.73$ $\eta = -0.36$ $\omega = -0.12$
Coverage of price index: 42 per cent

$\bar{R} = 0.30$

	Y'	V
P_t	-0.49	0.07
Y'		-0.51

1926–55 $X' = -1.05 + 0.13P_t + 0.01Y' - 0.07V$
           (0.07)   (0.01)   (0.35)
     $d = 0.67$ $\eta = 1.43$ $\omega = 0.41$
Coverage of price index: 42 per cent

$\bar{R} = 0.35$

	Y'	V
P_t	-0.77	-0.26
Y'		0.30

     $F(3, 16) = 20.90$: significant

Note the low coverage of the price index.

Automobiles

For reasons given in chapter III, least squares seemed to be an inappropriate method of estimating the coefficients of demand for this category. For automobiles only, Gigantes has formulated an over-identified linear model containing three equations and has obtained limited information estimates of the structural parameters.[1] The model is the following:

$$X^* + \alpha_{12}P''_h = \beta_{10} + \beta_{11}P''_i + \beta_{12}P''_c + \beta_{13}Y + \beta_{14}S + \epsilon_1$$

$$X^*_h + \alpha_{22}P''_h = \beta_{20} + \beta_{21}P''_i + \beta_{22}P''_c + \beta_{23}Y + \beta_{24}S + \epsilon_2$$

$$P''_h + \alpha_{33}X^*_h = \beta_{30} + \beta_{35}W + \beta_{36}X^*_x + \beta_{37}t + \epsilon_3.$$

The ϵ_i are unobserved random variables, assumed to be normally distributed with zero means. The first two equations relate the demand for imports and the demand for home-produced automobiles, respectively, to the usual variables plus the beginning stock.[2] The third equation relates the price of home-produced automobiles to production for export, production for the domestic market, a rough measure of costs, and a linear time trend. The three variables placed on the left-hand side are treated as endogenous variables, the remaining variables as exogenous.

The shortness of the postwar period ruled out separate estimates for the interwar and postwar periods. The following estimates were obtained by Gigantes from the data for 1926–39 and 1936–55, respectively.

1926–39 $X^* = 7.14 + 0.80P_i'' - 7.10P_h'' + 0.20P_c'' + 0.21\,Y - 0.04S$
                (1.80)   (3.60)   (3.50)   (0.06)   (0.02)

         $X^*_h = -368.59 - 7.80P_i'' + 23.90P_h'' + 30.00P_c'' + 0.03\,Y - 0.08S$
                  (7.60)   (19.90)   (17.40)   (0.29)   (0.08)

           $P_h'' = -0.19 - 0.06X^*_h + 0.10X^*_z + 1.06W + 0.04t$
                 (0.02)   (0.03)   (0.41)   (0.07)

              $\eta = 0.52$ $\eta' = -4.15$ $\omega = 4.87$

1926–55 $X^* = -17.92 - 3.30P_i'' - 2.70P_h'' + 8.20P_c'' + 0.05\,Y - 0.04S$
                (2.60)   (3.20)   (3.80)   (0.05)   (0.02)

         $X^*_h = 91.52 - 8.90P_i'' - 14.10P_h'' + 8.70P_c'' + 0.36\,Y - 0.02S$
               (4.70)   (5.90)   (6.90)   (0.10)   (0.04)

          $P_h'' = 44.03 - 0.05X^*_h - 0.07X^*_z - 1.18W + 0.03t$
           (0.01)   (0.01)   (0.07)   (0.03)

            $\eta = -1.91$ $\eta' = -1.44$ $\omega = 1.57$

The estimates evidently are far from satisfactory. Not only are they highly sensitive to changes in the sample—possibly the result of a wartime break in structure—but, in the case of the coefficients of prices and cost, they sometimes have the "wrong" sign. The high intercorrelations of the price indices $[r(P_i'', P_h'') = 0.98$ for 1926–55] no doubt provide one part of the explanation. And the third or price-forming equation undoubtedly could be improved. But it is likely that reliable estimates of the coefficients will remain beyond reach until data on the age distribution of automobiles and on the prices of second-hand automobiles become available.

Miscellaneous Consumer Goods

1926–39 $X' = 11.50 - 1.32P_i + 0.19\,Y'$ $\bar{R} = 0.99$
            (0.10)   (0.02)

        $d = 2.13$ $\eta = -2.48$ $\omega = 1.23$ $r(P_i, Y') = -0.45$
        Coverage of price index: 45 per cent

1947–55 $X' = 9.97 - 0.36P_i + 0.40\,Y' - 1.74V$ $\bar{R} = 0.88$
            (0.51)   (0.17)   (0.98)

        $d = 2.18$ $\eta = -0.47$ $\omega = 2.66$
        Coverage of price index: 42 per cent

	Y'	V
P_i	-0.52	-0.06
Y'		-0.51

1926–55 $X' = 6.90 - 1.01P_i + 0.24\,Y' - 2.36V$ $\bar{R} = 0.98$
            (0.14)   (0.01)   (0.50)

        $d = 2.08$ $\eta = -1.60$ $\omega = 1.56$
        Coverage of price index: 43 per cent

	Y'	V
P_i	0.70	0.27
Y'		0.30

        $F(3, 16) = 2.33$: not significant

The fit is gratifyingly close, but the low coverage of the price index should be borne in mind.

Machinery and Equipment

1926–39 $X = 142.64 - 20.86P_i' + 1.63G$ $\bar{R} = 0.94$
$\qquad\qquad (4.32) \qquad\quad (0.52)$
$\qquad d = 1.10 \quad \eta = -2.61 \quad \omega = 1.74$ $r(P_i', G) = -0.61$

1947–55 $X = -126.87 - 1.38P_i' + 2.75G$ $\bar{R} = 0.89$
$\qquad\qquad\quad (31.13) \qquad (0.54)$
$\qquad d = 2.70 \quad \eta = -0.29 \quad \omega = 1.38$ $r(P_i', G) = 0.29$

1926–55 $X = 0.30 - 14.30P_i' + 2.62G$ $\bar{R} = 0.99$
$\qquad\qquad (5.45) \qquad\quad (0.12)$
$\qquad d = 2.21 \quad \eta = -0.66 \quad \omega = 1.66$ $r(P_i', G) = -0.69$
$\qquad F(2, 18) = 1.10$: not significant

Materials for Investment in Structures (with Direct Price)

1926–39 $X = 86.87 - 9.14P_d' + 0.37G$ $\bar{R} = 0.95$
$\qquad\qquad (1.17) \qquad\quad (0.14)$
$\qquad d = 1.06 \quad \eta = -3.12 \quad \omega = 1.06$ $r(P_d', G) = -0.50$
$\qquad$ Coverage of price index: 22 per cent

1947–55 $X = -77.07 - 0.59P_d' + 0.90G$ $\bar{R} = 0.98$
$\qquad\qquad\quad (3.63) \qquad\quad (0.08)$
$\qquad d = 3.27 \quad \eta = -0.07 \quad \omega = 1.99$ $r(P_d', G) = 0.63$
$\qquad$ Coverage of price index: 40 per cent

1926–55 $X = 44.74 - 6.60P_d' + 0.57G$ $\bar{R} = 0.97$
$\qquad\qquad (1.78) \qquad\quad (0.03)$
$\qquad d = 0.52 \quad \eta = -1.28 \quad \omega = 1.39$ $r(P_d', G) = 0.03$
$\qquad$ Coverage of price index: 35 per cent
$\qquad F(2, 18) = 28.94$: significant

Materials for Investment in Structures (with Indirect Price)

1926–39 $X = 121.08 - 11.47P_i' + 0.24G$ $\bar{R} = 0.77$
$\qquad\qquad (4.32) \qquad\quad (0.36)$
$\qquad d = 0.60 \quad \eta = -3.97 \quad \omega = 0.68$ $r(P_i', G) = -0.72$
$\qquad$ Coverage of price index: 26 per cent

1947–55 $X = -80.34 - 0.09P_i' + 0.89G$ $\bar{R} = 0.98$
$\qquad\qquad\quad (2.19) \qquad\quad (0.07)$
$\qquad d = 3.23 \quad \eta = -0.01 \quad \omega = 1.97$ $r(P_i', G) = -0.45$
$\qquad$ Coverage of price index: 32 per cent

1926–55 $X = 57.33 - 7.18P_i' + 0.50G$ $\bar{R} = 0.96$
$\qquad\qquad (2.76) \qquad\quad (0.04)$
$\qquad d = 0.65 \quad \eta = -1.33 \quad \omega = 1.20$ $r(P_i', G) = -0.63$
$\qquad$ Coverage of price index: 30 per cent

$F(2, 18) = 6.85$: significant

$r(P_d', P_i') = 0.86$ for 1926–39

$\qquad\qquad\ \ = 0.10$ for 1947–55

$\qquad\qquad\ \ = 0.56$ for 1926–55

The coverage of both price indices is low. That at least one of them is unreliable is indicated by the low correlation between them in the postwar period. For all regressions the residuals are highly autocorrelated.

Unassigned Industrial Materials

1929–39　$X = -22.81 - 2.16P_i' + 1.84G$　　　　　　$\bar{R} = 0.81$

$\qquad\qquad\quad\ \ (2.54)\qquad\ (0.37)$

$\qquad\quad d = 1.52\quad \eta = -0.21\quad \omega = 1.43$　　　　$r(P_i', G) = 0.10$

$\qquad\quad$ Coverage of price index: 26 per cent

1947–55　$X = 71.99 - 3.55P_i' + 1.06G$　　　　　　$\bar{R} = 0.89$

$\qquad\qquad\quad\ \ (5.94)\qquad\ (0.21)$

$\qquad\quad d = 1.56\quad \eta = -0.13\quad \omega = 0.83$　　　　$r(P_i', G) = 0.20$

$\qquad\quad$ Coverage of price index: 27 per cent

1926–55　$X = 27.70 - 2.33P_i' + 1.24G$　　　　　　$\bar{R} = 0.98$

$\qquad\qquad\quad\ \ (2.30)\qquad\ (0.06)$

$\qquad\quad d = 1.50\quad \eta = -0.14\quad \omega = 0.96$　　　　$r(P_i', G) = -0.45$

$\qquad\quad$ Coverage of price index: 27 per cent

$\qquad\quad F(2, 18) = 1.84$: not significant

Note the extremely low coverage of the price index.

Petroleum and Petroleum Products

1926–39　$X = -71.46 - 0.41P_d' + 4.95P_h' + 0.92G$　　$\bar{R} = 0.71$

$\qquad\qquad\qquad\ \ (2.27)\qquad (1.68)\qquad (0.18)$

$\qquad\quad d = 1.24\quad \eta = -0.08\quad \eta' = 1.11\quad \omega = 1.57$

$\qquad\quad$ Coverage of direct price index: 87 per cent

	P_h'	G
P_d'	0.75	−0.71
P_h'		−0.66

1947–55　$X = 99.95 - 1.30P_d' - 6.02P_h' + 0.58G$　　$\bar{R} = 0.87$

$\qquad\qquad\qquad\ \ (5.49)\qquad (8.15)\qquad (0.09)$

$\qquad\quad d = 2.99\quad \eta = -0.07\quad \eta' = -0.31\quad \omega = 0.72$

$\qquad\quad$ Coverage of direct price index: 85 per cent

	P_h'	G
P_d'	0.63	−0.41
P_h'		−0.30

1926–55　$X = -63.88 + 1.08P_d' + 2.11P_h' + 1.01G$　　$\bar{R} = 0.98$

$\qquad\qquad\qquad\ \ (3.51)\qquad (2.86)\qquad (0.05)$

$\qquad\quad d = 0.98\quad \eta = 0.11\quad \eta' = 0.22\quad \omega = 1.41$

$\qquad\quad$ Coverage of direct price index: 86 per cent

	P_h'	G
P_d'	0.86	−0.73
P_h'		−0.79

$\qquad\quad F(3, 16) = 2.00$: not significant

The postwar drop in the marginal propensity to import is possibly explicable in terms of the sharply upward trend in local supply and a similar trend in national product.

Coal (with Direct Price)

1926–39 $X = -33.85 - 9.83P_d' + 11.81P_h' + 0.68G$ $\bar{R} = 0.68$
                 (2.49)   (6.68)   (0.44)

$d = 1.61$ $\eta = -2.16$ $\eta' = 2.69$ $\omega = 1.23$

Coverage of direct price index: 88 per cent

	P_h'	G
P_d'	0.82	−0.66
P_h'		−0.93

1947–55 $X = 222.28 - 0.34P_d' - 10.33P_h' - 0.43G$ $\bar{R} = 0.56$
                 (12.45)   (10.90)   (0.12)

$d = 3.31$ $\eta = -0.04$ $\eta' = -1.24$ $\omega = 1.29$

Coverage of direct price index: 93 per cent

	P_h'	G
P_d'	0.77	−0.30
P_h'		−0.50

1926–55 $X = 159.75 - 5.56P_d' - 5.10P_h' - 0.10G$ $\bar{R} = 0.62$
                 (3.48)   (4.82)   (0.09)

$d = 0.96$ $\eta = -0.97$ $\eta' = -0.90$ $\omega = -0.23$

Coverage of direct price index: 89 per cent

$F(3, 16) = 8.96$: significant

	P_h'	G
P_d'	0.92	−0.79
P_h'		−0.93

Coal (with Indirect Price)

1926–39 $X = -39.71 - 11.81P_i' + 13.06P_h' + 0.80G$ $\bar{R} = 0.79$
                 (2.21)   (5.36)   (0.36)

$d = 1.36$ $\eta = -2.53$ $\eta' = 2.98$ $\omega = 1.45$

Coverage of indirect price index: 92 per cent

	P_h'	G
P_i'	0.80	−0.63
P_h'		−0.93

1947–55 $X = 231.31 - 1.45P_i' - 9.68P_h' - 0.46G$ $\bar{R} = 0.75$
                 (11.86)   (10.10)   (0.22)

$d = 3.28$ $\eta = -0.20$ $\eta' = -1.16$ $\omega = -1.36$

Coverage of indirect price index: 95 per cent

	P_h'	G
P_i'	0.74	−0.86
P_h'		−0.50

1926–55 $X = 170.70 + 0.23P_i' - 11.35P_h' - 0.15G$ $\bar{R} = 0.76$
                 (3.19)   (3.93)   (0.09)

$d = 0.98$ $\eta = 0.04$ $\eta' = -2.01$ $\omega = -0.35$

Coverage of indirect price index: 93 per cent

	P_h'	G
P_i'	0.80	−0.69
P_h'		−0.93

$F(3, 16) = 13.29$: significant
$$r(P_d', P_i') = 0.98$$
$$r(P_d', P_i') = 0.70$$
$$r(P_d', P_i') = 0.94$$

Note the high correlation between the price of coal and the price of home-produced competing goods (petroleum, in this case) and the serious autocorrelation of the postwar residuals.

Fuels

1926–39 $X = 32.10 - 1.55P_d' + 0.92G$ $\bar{R} = 0.77$
                (2.49)   (0.22)
        $d = 0.81$ $\eta = -0.16$ $\omega = 0.81$ $r(P_d', G) = -0.73$
        Coverage of price index: 86 per cent

1947–55 $X = 300.06 - 14.29P_d' + 0.13G$ $\bar{R} = 0.19$
                (10.66)   (0.18)
        $d = 3.31$ $\eta = -0.56$ $\omega = 0.12$ $r(P_d', G) = -0.41$
        Coverage of price index: 87 per cent

1926–55 $X = 65.34 - 5.27P_d' + 0.98G$ $\bar{R} = 0.94$
                (4.93)   (0.09)
        $d = 0.85$ $\eta = -0.35$ $\omega = 0.87$ $r(P_d', G) = -0.78$
        Coverage of price index: 86 per cent
        $F(2, 18) = 29.32$: significant

From a comparison of the estimates of the price elasticities for the petroleum and petroleum products, coal, and fuels categories, one might have expected to have drawn some conclusions concerning the sign and magnitude of the aggregation bias referred to in the introduction. But the high standard errors and marked autocorrelation of the residuals, especially in the postwar period, preclude any confident inferences. About the only conclusion that emerges is that the estimates for the interwar period lend some slender support to the hypothesis that the bias is "towards zero," both for the price elasticity and for the income elasticity.

Total Imports

1926–39 $X = 2272.37 - 207.62P_i' + 5.15G$ $\bar{R} = 0.93$
                (50.23)   (2.56)
        $d = 1.62$ $\eta = -3.18$ $\omega = 0.65$ $r(P_i', G) = -0.77$

1947–55 $X = -1506.04 + 111.72P_i' + 10.09G$ $\bar{R} = 0.97$
                (45.29)   (0.85)
        $d = 1.20$ $\eta = 0.75$ $\omega = 1.30$ $r(P_i', G) = -0.44$

1926–55 $X = 926.94 - 91.38P_i' + 7.58G$ $\bar{R} = 0.98$
                (38.99)   (0.34)
        $d = 1.35$ $\eta = -0.93$ $\omega = 0.96$ $r(P_i', G) = -0.35$
        $F(2, 18) = 13.86$: significant

Note that our earlier (chapter III) defence of least squares does not extend to the aggregate of all imports.

The price and income elasticities are brought together in Tables 4.1 and 4.2.

TABLE 4.1

PRICE ELASTICITIES OF DEMAND FOR IMPORTS

	1926–55	1926–39	1947–55
Consumers' goods			
Furniture, household appliances, etc.	−1.45*	−4.10	−0.03*
Food and food materials—direct price	−0.77	−0.67*	0.50*
—indirect price	−0.32*	−0.34*	0.14*
Clothing and textiles, etc.	1.25	−0.18*	0.91*
Beverages and tobacco	1.43*	1.55	−0.36*
Automobiles	−1.91*	0.52*	
Miscellaneous consumers' goods	−1.60	−2.48	−0.47*
Producers' goods			
Machinery and equipment	−0.66	−2.61	−0.29*
Materials for investment in structures—direct price	−1.28	−3.12	−0.07*
—indirect price	−1.33	−3.97	−0.01*
Unassigned industrial materials	−0.14*	−0.21*	−0.13*
Petroleum and petroleum products	0.11*	−0.08*	−0.07*
Coal—direct price	−0.37*	−2.16	−0.04*
—indirect price	0.04*	−2.53	−0.20*
Fuels	−0.35*	−0.16*	−0.56*
Total imports	−0.93	−3.18	0.75

*Not significant at 5 per cent level.

TABLE 4.2

INCOME ELASTICITIES OF DEMAND FOR IMPORTS

	1926–55	1926–39	1947–55
Consumers' goods			
Furniture, household appliances, etc.	3.10	2.47	7.65
Food and food materials—direct price	5.77	2.70*	−2.48*
—indirect price	7.44	4.11*	−3.17*
Clothing and textiles, etc.	0.31*	1.62*	−1.38*
Beverages and tobacco	0.41*	3.84	−0.12*
Automobiles	1.57*	4.87	
Miscellaneous consumers' goods	1.56	1.23	2.66*
Producers' goods			
Machinery and equipment	1.66	1.74	1.38
Materials for investment in structures—direct price	1.39	1.06	1.99
—indirect price	1.20	0.68*	1.97
Unassigned industrial materials	0.96	1.43	0.83
Petroleum and petroleum products	1.41	1.57	0.72
Coal—direct price	−0.23*	1.23*	−1.29
—indirect price	−0.35*	1.45*	−1.36*
Fuels	0.87	0.81	0.12*
Total imports	0.96	0.65*	1.30

*Not significant at the 5 per cent level.

PART B: COMMENTS ON THE ESTIMATES

The estimates are of very mixed value. Fluctuations in the volume of certain types of imports—for example, miscellaneous consumers' goods, machinery and equipment, and materials for investment in structures—proved to be amenable to relatively complete explanations in terms of the movements of an income or output variable and a single price variable. Other categories proved more elusive. Beverages and tobacco; clothing and textiles, etc.; automobiles, trucks, and parts;

and the three fuels categories proved especially intractable. In the case of some categories—for example, beverages and tobacco, and clothing and textiles—the difficulties may stem from the unreliability of the price series used. In the case of automobiles, trucks, and parts the gaps in our information are even more serious. It is doubtful whether appreciably better estimates will be obtained until reliable series of liquid assets, at least for households, are constructed and until the age distribution of automobiles and trucks for a succession of years is available.

Even in the case of those categories for which good fits were obtained, the estimates should not be taken too seriously. The appropriateness of the method of least squares has been argued in chapter III. But errors of observation, the low coverage of some of the price indices and the reliance on just two or three explanatory variables make it highly likely that the estimates are biased. (The sign of the bias arising from the use of imperfect price indices is shown in appendix v to be predictable and to depend on the type of index employed.) Finally, the small number of postwar observations makes for highly unreliable results.

Subject to these important reservations, a couple of tentative generalizations are ventured. First, the results summarized in Tables 4.1 and 4.2 suggest that the role of price in the balance of payments adjustment mechanism may be greater than earlier studies for Canada and for other countries had suggested.[3] In the interwar period the estimated coefficient of import price was significantly different from zero for six categories out of twelve. For five of those six categories the elasticity was algebraically less than minus two. It is possible that in earlier studies the price elasticity was obscured by the high degree of aggregation. That estimates of the price elasticity derived from aggregative data tend to be biased towards zero has been suggested in chapter I, and is indeed well known. Our results suggest that, at least for Canada, the bias may be quantitatively important, that is, large relative to the true values of the slopes.

Second, for five out of the ten independent categories[4] for which the test of structural break could be applied[5] there was evidence of a wartime break in structure. The five categories were food and food materials; beverages and tobacco; furniture, household appliances, etc.; coal; and materials for investment in structures. In all five cases the estimate of the price elasticity of demand is smaller in absolute value in the postwar period than in the prewar period.[6] The evidence is too slender to support a confident generalization. But it does suggest that Canadian imports may have become less sensitive to price changes.[7] The relevance of such a change for tariff and exchange rate policy would depend on the magnitude of the change. For the five categories concerned, the change appears to be substantial, but it would be foolish to make much of the evidence turned up so far.[8]

CHAPTER FIVE

THE DIRECTION OF FUTURE RESEARCH

THE SERIES and estimates provided in this book represent, I think, an improvement over what is now available. It should be emphasized, however, that the series still embody a substantial degree of aggregation, not only over commodities but also over time (the data are annual) and over sources of supply. The time disaggregation of the price and quantity series is clearly essential to the study of the short-run responses of demand to changes in price and income. But the basic sources of data are such that there is little hope of improvement in this direction in the foreseeable future. On the other hand, it is possible to construct from published sources separate price and quantity series for each of the major sources of supply, the United Kingdom and the United States. Indeed, an important beginning has already been made by Parizeau and Reuber, whose work will be outlined below.[1]

The importance of obtaining separate price and quantity series for imports from the United States and from the United Kingdom need not be laboured. Not only do the two countries provide qualitatively different kinds of commodities, but tariff and exchange rate adjustments have rarely been non-discriminatory.[2]

The most ambitious attack on the problem of constructing price and quantity series by country of origin is that of Jacques Parizeau.[3] In his University of London doctoral dissertation he presented quantity and Paasche-type f.o.b. price series for imports from both the United Kingdom and the United States—for the fiscal years 1927–28 to 1938–39 in the case of the United States, from 1928–29 to 1938–39 for the United Kingdom. In addition, he has provided, in graphic form, price and quantity series for certain subgroups of aggregate imports (non-metallic minerals, iron and steel, textiles). Finally, he has provided, in both graphic and tabular form, price and quantity series for imports of two important individual commodities (unbleached cotton, anthracite) from each country.

It appears from Parizeau's figures that the over-all indices of the prices of imports from the United States and from the United Kingdom moved more or less in step during the period covered, the ratio U.K. prices : U.S. prices ranging from 96.0 per cent to 104.2 per cent. But the corresponding sectional price ratios varied within much wider limits, and the ratios of prices for individual commodities varied quite remarkably—unbleached cotton from 42.9 per cent to 90.3 per cent, anthracite from 97.9 per cent to 137.9 per cent.

The chief drawback of Parizeau's data, from the point of view of demand estimation, is that the price data are f.o.b. *Ad valorem* rates of duty can be computed, as can rates of local taxes. The chief gap in our information relates to freight rates. Parizeau provides a number of helpful suggestions in this connection, but does not follow them up. Another difficulty with Parizeau's data stems from his decision to represent in his indices only those imports which were supplied by both the United States and the United Kingdom. Finally, his series covers a period of only eleven years, rather short for purposes of estimation.

Longer price series, but for aggregate imports from the United Kingdom only, have recently been published by G. L. Reuber.[4]

APPENDIXES AND NOTES

STATISTICAL SERIES

IN THIS APPENDIX are assembled the basic time series of price, quantity, income, and output from which the estimates set out in chapter IV were derived. The manner in which the import price series were constructed has been described in chapter II and in appendix III.

The Consumer Price Index and the Wholesale Price Index, both of which are employed as deflators, have been taken from the *Canadian Statistical Review Supplement 1956*.

In several regressions, an index of the prices of domestically produced substitutes has been introduced. In the case of the food and food materials regressions, the food component of the Consumer Price Index was used. In the clothing and textiles, etc. regressions the clothing component of the Consumer Price Index was used. In the coal regressions the petroleum products component of the Wholesale Price Index was used. In the petroleum and petroleum products regressions the coal component of the wholesale price index was used. Finally in the automobiles, trucks, and parts regressions an unpublished DBS series based on the prices of new Ford, Plymouth, and Chevrolet automobiles was used. It is the replacement component of the automobile costs group of the Consumer Price Index.

The series for disposable personal income and for gross national product have been taken from *National Accounts Income and Expenditure 1926–58* (Ottawa 1958).

The stock of automobiles series was constructed by Gigantes[1] in the following way. For any given year take 75 per cent of sales (including imports) in the previous year and add to that 65 per cent of sales two years ago, 55 per cent of sales three years ago, etc., until the seventh year is reached. Then add 5 per cent of the cars registered eight years ago. For the period before 1932 no sales figures are available and "apparent consumption" is substituted.[2] Only rough DBS estimates of apparent consumption are available for the period 1921–24.[3] The figures used for 1919 and 1920 are guesses arrived at by crude extrapolation.

TABLE I.1
FOOD AND FOOD MATERIALS

Year	Value ($ million)	Quantity (millions of 1936 dollars)	Quantity ——— Population	F.O.B. price (1936 = 10)	Direct price (1936 = 10)
1926	158.80	98.09	10.38	16.19	12.65
1927	170.80	101.90	10.57	16.77	12.98
1928	202.60	123.31	12.54	16.43	12.70
1929	208.10	140.61	14.02	14.80	11.79
1930	159.00	116.31	11.40	13.67	11.29
1931	101.50	98.16	9.46	10.34	9.51
1932	76.50	80.70	7.68	9.48	9.37
1933	70.40	79.37	7.46	8.87	9.55
1934	85.20	88.47	8.23	9.63	9.90
1935	91.60	91.88	8.48	9.97	9.70
1936	107.70	107.70	9.84	10.00	10.00
1937	121.87	108.52	9.82	11.23	11.22
1938	109.47	115.23	10.34	9.50	9.35
1939	111.10	119.85	10.64	9.27	10.11
1946	286.76	137.27	11.16	20.89	15.71
1947	336.20	137.70	10.98	24.41	19.89
1948	329.10	128.91	9.78	26.25	23.90
1949	338.39	127.79	9.50	26.48	22.57
1950	436.44	149.26	10.89	29.24	24.18
1951	487.40	147.25	10.51	33.10	26.32
1952	438.60	156.20	10.80	28.08	24.22
1953	434.00	164.02	11.05	26.46	23.55
1954	501.60	173.56	11.35	28.90	27.41
1955	508.10	187.98	11.98	27.03	24.69

Year	Indirect price (1936 = 10)	Direct price deflated by consumer price index (1936 = 10)	Indirect price deflated by consumer price index (1936 = 10)	Price of home-produced competing goods deflated by consumer price index (1936 = 10)	Tariff rates (per cent)
1926	16.23	10.19	13.07	11.15	15.55
1927	16.32	10.63	13.37	10.96	13.15
1928	15.69	10.34	12.78	10.94	11.38
1929	14.29	9.50	11.51	11.08	11.95
1930	13.55	9.16	11.00	10.91	12.86
1931	10.59	8.56	9.53	9.47	17.53
1932	9.38	9.28	9.29	8.68	19.56
1933	9.35	9.93	9.72	9.01	20.54
1934	10.03	10.15	10.29	9.71	18.98
1935	10.10	9.90	10.31	9.87	16.15
1936	10.00	10.00	10.00	10.00	13.92
1937	11.36	10.88	11.02	10.21	12.93
1938	9.67	8.96	9.27	10.15	14.48
1939	9.37	9.78	9.06	9.95	14.31
1946					7.42
1947	24.00	14.33	17.29	11.74	9.53
1948	24.03	15.05	15.13	12.58	4.33
1949	24.33	13.79	14.86	12.52	6.54
1950	26.16	14.36	15.53	12.48	5.47
1951	30.82	14.14	16.56	12.89	6.20
1952	25.78	12.70	13.52	12.55	6.94
1953	24.15	12.46	12.78	12.21	7.18
1954	26.22	14.41	13.79	12.09	6.64
1955	25.26	12.96	13.26	12.06	6.95

TABLE I.2

BEVERAGES AND TOBACCO

Year	Value ($ million)	Quantity (millions of 1936 dollars)	Quantity —— Population	F.O.B. price (1936=10)	Indirect price (1936=10)	Indirect price deflated by consumer price index (1936=10)	Tariff rates (per cent)
1926	21.10	12.22	1.29	17.27	16.96	13.66	80.33
1927	27.50	16.72	1.73	16.45	16.69	13.67	87.85
1928	30.10	19.95	2.03	15.09	15.98	13.01	89.90
1929	26.90	16.90	1.68	15.92	16.76	13.51	98.48
1930	21.40	14.03	1.38	15.25	16.19	13.14	102.76
1931	16.00	11.43	1.10	14.00	14.95	13.46	101.12
1932	10.10	7.29	.69	13.86	14.22	14.08	88.71
1933	8.10	6.30	.59	12.85	12.99	13.50	84.44
1934	8.30	6.00	.56	13.83	13.60	13.95	79.40
1935	9.30	7.18	.66	12.95	11.42	11.65	60.75
1936	10.10	10.10	.92	10.00	10.00	10.00	78.51
1937	11.49	10.29	.93	11.17	11.55	11.20	81.63
1938	12.15	10.54	.95	11.53	11.26	10.80	73.25
1939	9.50	10.35	.92	9.18	10.83	10.47	108.63
1946	17.97	11.91	.97	15.09			74.79
1947	17.60	12.53	1.00	14.05	15.88	11.44	86.07
1948	19.70	11.49	.90	17.15	16.31	10.27	59.34
1949	26.85	15.29	1.14	17.56	15.75	9.62	52.10
1950	21.66	11.79	.86	18.39	16.85	10.01	56.69
1951	22.70	12.52	.89	18.13	18.85	10.13	72.24
1952	25.80	15.59	1.08	16.55	18.04	9.46	83.29
1953	26.10	15.11	1.02	17.27	18.59	9.84	82.64
1954	25.00	14.29	.94	17.50	18.14	9.54	75.24
1955	25.80	15.18	.96	17.03	18.03	9.46	76.40

TABLE I.3

CLOTHING AND TEXTILES, PERSONAL FURNISHINGS, AND MATERIALS FOR SUCH USES

Year	Value ($ million)	Quantity (millions of 1936 dollars)	Quantity ———— Population	F.O.B. price (1936=10)	Indirect price (1936=10)	Indirect price deflated by consumer price index (1936=10)	Price of home-produced competing goods (1936=10)	Tariff rates (per cent)
1926	222.30	140.34	14.85	15.84	15.58	12.54	11.14	14.63
1927	229.00	151.46	15.71	15.12	14.79	12.11	10.62	15.00
1928	244.60	149.69	15.22	16.34	15.62	12.72	10.65	14.50
1929	242.10	153.81	15.33	15.74	14.96	12.05	10.18	14.15
1930	181.10	162.28	15.89	11.16	10.69	8.68	9.19	15.86
1931	112.40	129.34	12.46	8.69	8.83	7.95	9.14	20.09
1932	84.70	106.27	10.11	7.97	8.07	7.99	9.55	16.99
1933	87.00	101.05	9.50	8.61	8.65	8.99	10.03	15.34
1934	102.90	107.75	10.03	9.55	9.44	9.68	10.34	13.41
1935	106.90	111.94	10.32	9.55	9.41	9.60	10.02	13.01
1936	126.00	126.00	11.51	10.00	10.00	10.00	10.00	11.84
1937	144.80	129.63	11.85	11.06	11.15	10.81	10.08	10.82
1938	113.20	98.18	10.84	9.36	9.31	8.93	9.03	12.38
1939	134.50	146.51	12.58	9.48	9.41	9.10	9.43	11.04
1946	322.70	175.48	14.27	18.39				10.65
1947	463.30	212.23	16.91	21.83	22.44	16.17	12.75	12.27
1948	408.30	164.97	12.86	24.75	23.97	15.09	13.43	7.62
1949	409.40	167.92	12.49	24.38	23.71	14.48	13.40	9.08
1950	451.50	171.48	12.51	26.33	25.25	15.00	14.45	8.39
1951	585.00	159.57	11.39	36.66	35.84	19.26	15.68	7.77
1952	456.80	177.26	12.26	25.77	25.88	13.57	13.00	10.78
1953	496.50	204.91	13.81	24.23	24.52	12.97	12.47	12.06
1954	433.70	182.15	11.92	23.81	24.16	12.70	11.98	12.01
1955	498.50	213.31	13.59	23.37	24.07	12.64	11.71	11.95

TABLE I.4

FURNITURE, HOUSEHOLD APPLIANCES, RADIO AND TELEVISION

Year	Value ($ million)	Quantity (millions of 1936 dollars)	Quantity Population	F.O.B. price (1936 = 10)	Indirect price (1936 = 10)	Indirect price deflated by consumer price index (1936 = 10)	Tariff rates (per cent)
1926	7.62	6.20	.66	12.30	12.06	10.03	27.43
1927	9.04	7.64	.79	11.84	11.63	9.52	28.43
1928	13.73	11.65	1.19	11.79	11.06	9.01	24.25
1929	20.22	16.49	1.65	12.26	11.39	9.18	24.53
1930	16.60	14.63	1.44	11.35	10.65	8.64	27.59
1931	11.32	10.61	1.02	10.67	10.18	9.16	27.56
1932	3.91	3.81	.36	10.27	10.64	10.53	35.29
1933	3.15	3.19	.30	9.89	10.01	10.41	30.79
1934	4.35	4.47	.41	9.73	9.76	10.01	29.20
1935	5.52	5.59	.52	9.87	9.58	9.78	25.18
1936	6.78	6.78	.62	10.00	10.00	10.00	26.84
1937	11.84	10.63	.96	11.14	10.81	10.48	21.14
1938	11.84	10.39	.97	10.89	10.11	9.69	17.15
1939	10.12	9.15	.81	11.06	10.73	10.38	23.02
1946	34.39	21.79	1.77	15.78			15.46
1947	60.80	34.68	2.76	17.53	17.66	12.72	19.78
1948	27.20	14.31	1.12	19.01	19.99	12.59	17.90
1949	43.40	22.05	1.64	19.68	17.80	10.87	13.73
1950	61.34	29.85	2.18	20.55	18.61	11.05	15.10
1951	89.50	40.24	2.87	22.24	22.92	12.32	15.50
1952	107.74	49.49	3.42	21.77	21.12	11.07	15.59
1953	157.60	71.21	4.80	22.13	20.29	10.74	14.59
1954	132.90	59.77	3.91	22.24	20.86	10.97	17.12
1955	160.70	70.73	4.51	22.72	21.23	11.14	14.82

TABLE I.5

MISCELLANEOUS CONSUMER GOODS

Year	Value ($ million)	Quantity (millions of 1936 dollars)	Quantity Population	F.O.B. price (1936=10)	Indirect price (1936=10)	Indirect price deflated by consumer price index (1936=10)	Tariff rates (per cent)
1926	63.65	54.59	5.78	11.66	11.61	9.35	19.78
1927	69.61	59.60	6.18	11.68	11.48	9.40	19.36
1928	72.37	64.73	6.58	11.18	11.04	8.99	21.13
1929	78.87	71.24	7.10	11.07	10.88	8.77	21.47
1930	78.91	75.30	7.46	10.48	9.88	8.02	18.30
1931	57.27	55.23	5.32	10.37	10.01	9.01	19.54
1932	42.97	42.58	4.05	10.09	9.95	9.85	19.30
1933	33.81	34.18	3.23	9.85	9.91	10.30	20.66
1934	36.04	35.97	3.35	10.02	10.03	10.29	19.45
1935	40.26	40.70	3.75	9.89	9.90	10.10	19.78
1936	47.67	47.67	4.36	10.00	10.00	10.00	17.86
1937	57.62	53.55	4.84	10.76	10.55	10.23	13.72
1938	56.10	52.97	4.75	10.59	10.54	10.11	16.40
1939	56.31	52.28	4.64	10.77	10.55	10.22	15.00
1946	140.41	88.48	7.20	15.87			15.70
1947	177.95	101.22	8.07	17.58	17.85	12.86	15.72
1948	148.98	80.75	6.30	18.45	17.88	11.26	11.42
1949	182.28	95.99	7.14	18.99	18.53	11.32	11.74
1950	196.88	99.84	7.28	19.72	19.09	11.34	13.20
1951	257.32	115.29	8.23	22.32	22.29	11.98	13.06
1952	284.80	135.88	9.40	20.96	20.54	10.77	12.00
1953	317.87	151.15	10.18	21.03	20.91	11.06	14.34
1954	341.31	164.33	10.75	20.77	20.48	10.77	13.15
1955	477.00	182.30	10.19	20.68	20.64	10.83	13.26

TABLE I.6

AUTOMOBILES, TRUCKS, AND PARTS

Year	Value ($ million)	Quantity (millions of 1936 dollars)	F.O.B. price (1936 = 10)	Indirect price (1936 = 10)	Indirect price deflated by consumer price index (1936 = 10)	Tariff rates (per cent)
1926	61.43	51.19	12.00	12.25	9.86	27.59
1927	75.74	65.75	11.52	11.48	9.40	25.38
1928	101.18	86.92	11.64	11.88	9.67	29.74
1929	93.38	77.24	12.09	11.61	9.36	23.42
1930	49.60	43.89	11.30	10.90	8.85	24.86
1931	27.34	24.43	11.19	10.97	9.87	25.38
1932	17.53	14.78	11.86	11.72	11.60	23.62
1933	15.42	14.34	10.91	11.33	11.78	28.73
1934	26.93	25.84	10.42	10.57	10.84	25.36
1935	33.57	33.11	10.14	9.88	10.08	20.16
1936	36.83	36.83	10.00	10.00	10.00	19.44
1937	54.69	51.06	10.71	10.21	9.90	13.69
1938	38.53	33.45	11.52	11.03	10.58	13.60
1939	43.18	37.10	11.64	11.10	10.74	14.45
1946	105.10	63.16	16.64			18.25
1947	178.40	99.22	17.98	18.91	13.62	17.29
1948	138.40	70.04	19.76	21.98	13.84	13.59
1949	174.80	83.44	20.95	20.45	12.49	10.15
1950	262.60	116.09	22.62	22.13	13.14	9.80
1951	287.90	125.28	22.98	25.34	13.62	13.29
1952	270.40	120.02	22.83	24.76	12.98	13.22
1953	340.20	148.62	22.89	24.17	12.79	12.66
1954	276.40	122.25	22.61	23.85	12.54	12.45
1955	388.80	164.89	23.58	24.97	13.11	12.97

TABLE I.7

AUTOMOBILES ONLY

Year	Value of imports ($ million)	Value of home-produced automobiles sold in Canada* ($ million)	Value of exports ($ million)	Price of exports† (1936=10)	Indirect price (1936=10)
1926	21.56	121.41	25.78	10.91	12.13
1927	26.90	118.97	22.16	10.05	11.49
1928	32.53	154.04	25.22	10.36	11.39
1929	32.60	157.32	29.82	10.30	11.39
1930	15.90	94.38	12.74	9.60	10.70
1931	5.77	58.30	4.01	9.80	11.18
1932	0.92	37.08	4.28	9.72	12.86
1933	1.17	37.35	6.81	9.51	9.91
1934	1.21	61.15	12.99	9.17	10.20
1935	1.94	79.55	16.89	9.17	9.88
1936	5.66	84.04	15.29	10.00	10.00
1937	11.93	93.03	15.92	10.02	10.55
1938	9.59	85.38	15.31	10.36	10.88
1939	11.72	73.69	14.39	10.26	11.35
1947	48.10	186.99	33.58	18.91	19.83
1948	18.82	245.26	20.90	20.24	20.76
1949	37.47	337.36	15.89	23.85	19.40
1950	74.96	511.75	19.38	23.64	20.60
1951	55.67	571.84	38.49	25.22	25.92
1952	47.13	630.91	43.63	25.42	24.40
1953	77.64	744.45	36.06	25.61	23.97
1954	58.57	680.41	7.72	25.47	24.03
1955	78.93	865.49	13.16	24.78	25.82

*DBS, *Motor Vehicles*.
†DBS, Unpublished.

Year	Price of home-produced automobiles* (1936=10)	Quantity of imports (millions of 1936 dollars)	Quantity of home-produced automobiles sold in Canada (millions of 1936 dollars)	Quantity of exports (millions of 1936 dollars)
1926	9.62	17.97	126.21	23.63
1927	8.64	23.35	137.69	20.05
1928	9.01	27.95	171.11	24.34
1929	9.56	26.96	164.56	28.95
1930	9.37	14.07	100.72	13.27
1931	8.64	5.16	67.48	4.09
1932	9.22	0.78	40.22	4.40
1933	9.12	1.07	40.95	7.16
1934	9.64	1.16	63.43	14.17
1935	10.02	1.91	79.39	18.42
1936	10.00	5.66	84.04	15.29
1937	9.83	11.14	94.64	15.89
1938	10.84	8.32	79.18	14.78
1939	10.63	10.07	69.32	14.03
1947	17.23	26.75	108.53	17.76
1948	19.66	9.52	124.75	10.33
1949	20.96	17.89	160.95	6.66
1950	21.13	33.14	242.19	8.19
1951	24.19	24.23	236.40	15.26
1952	24.70	20.64	255.43	17.16
1953	24.28	33.92	306.61	14.08
1954	24.38	25.90	279.09	3.03
1955	22.60	33.47	382.96	5.31

*See introduction to this appendix.

TABLE I.7 (*continued*)

Year	Index of wages in manufacturing industry in Canada (1936=10)	Automobiles registered on March 31* (in hundreds of thousands)	Stock of automobiles†
1926	10.42	6.41	212.5
1927	10.56	7.37	274.6
1928	10.64	8.30	328.3
1929	10.71	9.31	406.5
1930	10.71	10.23	466.2
1931	10.44	10.56	469.4
1932	9.76	10.24	426.3
1933	9.29	9.45	363.5
1934	9.56	9.17	305.7
1935	9.76	9.52	274.2
1936	10.00	9.90	265.0
1937	10.78	10.42	272.3
1938	11.12	11.03	304.9
1939	11.22	11.94	322.7
1947	20.56	12.39	164.8
1948	23.11	13.42	252.6
1949	24.45	15.04	325.3
1950	25.94	16.72	432.3
1951	29.41	19.10	615.5
1952	31.39	20.95	729.7
1953	32.91	22.96	828.7
1954	33.86	25.13	950.1
1955	34.77	26.83	1005.8

*DBS, *Car Registrations*.
†See introduction to this appendix.

TABLE I.7 (*continued*)

Year	Number of cars imported (thousands)	Number of cars produced and sold in Canada (thousands)	Number of cars exported (thousands)
1926	26.3	113.3	53.6
1927	32.8	106.5	39.9
1928	40.2	142.1	55.7
1929	39.4	138.4	64.9
1930	19.7	92.5	28.8
1931	7.5	55.8	9.3
1932	1.2	37.5	9.8
1933	1.1	38.5	15.8
1934	2.0	59.5	31.3
1935	3.1	80.1	47.6
1936	8.1	84.2	42.4
1937	17.3	97.0	43.8
1938	13.4	82.3	40.4
1939	16.6	74.5	38.5
1947	35.6	123.6	41.6
1948	17.0	128.6	27.3
1949	35.3	167.0	17.5
1950	81.7	243.2	24.1
1951	42.6	233.1	37.2
1952	34.7	257.4	41.7
1953	53.2	306.0	28.0
1954	38.5	272.0	7.3
1955	48.5	338.4	11.9

SOURCE: Canadian Automobile Chamber of Commerce, *Facts and Figures of the Automotive Industry* (Toronto, 1959), pp. 3, 13, 37. Figures for domestic sales are unavailable for the period 1926–32; for those years apparent domestic consumption (calculated as production less exports) is substituted. The maximum error involved in this approximation depends on the variability of inventories. On this there is no direct evidence.

TABLE I.8

MACHINERY AND EQUIPMENT

Year	Value ($ million)	Quantity (millions of 1936 dollars)	F.O.B. price (1936 = 10)	Indirect price (1936 = 10)	Indirect price deflated by wholesale price index (1936 = 10)	Price of home-produced competing goods deflated by wholesale price index (1936 = 10)	Tariff rates (per cent)
1926	91.23	79.19	11.52	11.22	8.34	8.17	21.25
1927	107.46	97.34	11.04	10.66	8.11	8.06	21.00
1928	148.00	134.18	11.03	10.39	8.00	8.12	19.52
1929	167.70	146.21	11.47	10.59	8.23	8.37	18.53
1930	121.30	113.90	10.65	9.73	8.34	8.87	19.08
1931	59.80	57.78	10.35	9.97	10.27	10.22	23.71
1932	33.99	32.50	10.46	10.25	11.41	11.03	23.36
1933	26.34	26.58	9.91	9.92	10.99	10.85	24.60
1934	33.61	34.47	9.75	9.87	10.23	10.06	25.52
1935	41.53	41.74	9.95	10.06	10.32	10.16	22.27
1936	54.73	54.73	10.00	10.00	10.00	10.00	18.41
1937	97.60	89.38	10.92	10.75	9.66	9.60	14.03
1938	86.90	79.29	10.96	10.00	9.49	10.15	11.06
1939	88.00	79.28	11.10	10.31	10.06	10.40	13.10
1946	294.32	218.50	13.47				12.13
1947	459.00	294.42	15.59	14.28	8.46	8.65	13.74
1948	511.20	288.81	17.70	14.53	7.27	8.25	9.42
1949	674.90	357.66	18.87	15.70	7.66	8.51	7.61
1950	570.10	280.29	20.34	17.00	7.79	8.54	9.60
1951	793.00	366.11	21.66	18.70	7.54	8.43	9.63
1952	862.70	417.37	20.67	17.80	7.62	8.91	11.62
1953	975.80	460.50	21.19	17.75	7.79	9.31	9.64
1954	910.70	426.96	21.33	18.33	8.18	9.71	12.24
1955	1005.70	453.43	22.18	19.03	8.42	9.78	10.61

TABLE I.9

MATERIALS FOR INVESTMENT IN STRUCTURES

Year	Value ($ million)	Quantity (millions of 1936 dollars)	F.O.B. price (1936 = 10)	Indirect price (1936 = 10)	Direct price deflated by wholesale price index (1936 = 10)	Direct price (1936 = 10)	Indirect price deflated by wholesale price index (1936 = 10)	Tariff rates (per cent)
1926	43.00	33.91	12.68	12.30	8.57	11.54	9.14	11.02
1927	47.10	38.36	12.28	11.64	8.11	10.67	8.85	10.28
1928	58.30	48.46	12.03	11.35	7.91	10.27	8.74	11.23
1929	67.40	54.71	12.32	11.47	8.13	10.46	8.91	11.08
1930	48.80	41.64	11.72	10.82	8.63	10.06	9.28	12.50
1931	27.70	26.38	10.50	10.47	10.25	9.95	10.78	14.62
1932	13.40	13.05	10.27	10.01	11.27	10.12	11.15	14.03
1933	10.70	10.52	10.17	10.02	11.10	10.02	11.10	14.11
1934	15.80	16.07	9.83	9.58	10.47	10.10	9.93	11.77
1935	17.90	18.32	9.77	9.45	10.13	9.88	9.69	12.40
1936	21.60	21.60	10.00	10.00	10.00	10.00	10.00	12.68
1937	30.34	27.81	10.91	10.87	9.91	11.03	9.77	9.06
1938	22.70	21.66	10.48	10.06	10.38	10.94	9.54	11.33
1939	27.80	25.09	11.08	9.86	10.64	10.91	9.62	10.00
1946	60.30	39.70	15.19			14.60		12.95
1947	103.30	56.79	18.19	17.88	9.89	16.68	10.60	12.86
1948	106.10	54.95	19.31	18.05	9.25	18.49	9.03	10.61
1949	135.60	68.94	19.67	17.59	9.67	19.81	8.58	8.48
1950	149.70	72.74	20.58	18.14	9.24	20.17	8.31	9.06
1951	207.40	89.51	23.17	21.34	9.02	22.39	8.60	8.73
1952	206.30	94.07	21.93	19.46	9.97	23.28	8.33	8.90
1953	224.60	102.89	21.83	19.15	10.23	23.33	8.40	9.18
1954	223.60	102.57	21.80	19.23	10.31	23.12	8.58	9.29
1955	264.50	114.55	23.09	20.56	10.32	23.34	9.09	7.88

TABLE I.10

UNASSIGNED INDUSTRIAL MATERIALS

Year	Value ($ million)	Quantity (millions of 1936 dollars)	F.O.B. price (1936 = 10)	Indirect price (1936 = 10)	Indirect price deflated by wholesale price index (1936 = 10)	Tariff rates (per cent)
1926	173.02	88.46	19.56	19.16	14.23	8.39
1927	168.17	104.98	16.02	15.04	11.44	7.24
1928	149.89	112.45	13.33	12.56	9.68	7.60
1929	171.20	140.67	12.17	11.72	9.11	10.27
1930	139.54	134.04	10.41	11.61	9.96	10.59
1931	86.72	102.87	8.43	8.32	8.57	10.80
1932	65.09	78.52	8.29	8.21	9.14	9.45
1933	56.00	67.80	8.26	8.25	9.14	9.25
1934	75.10	81.45	9.22	9.19	9.52	9.45
1935	100.90	109.67	9.20	9.04	9.27	7.69
1936	103.80	103.80	10.00	10.00	10.00	8.45
1937	144.80	124.94	11.59	11.67	10.49	7.86
1938	96.10	95.24	10.09	10.37	9.84	8.33
1939	125.10	117.24	10.67	10.58	10.32	7.35
1946	243.45	178.88	13.61			8.53
1947	305.60	211.93	14.42	15.32	9.08	3.93
1948	330.60	216.22	15.29	16.28	8.15	9.79
1949	211.90	211.93	15.73	16.20	7.91	8.71
1950	383.93	203.36	18.88	18.37	8.42	5.75
1951	584.98	233.71	25.03	25.21	10.16	5.55
1952	525.80	265.56	19.80	19.00	8.14	2.05
1953	516.40	276.15	18.70	18.74	8.22	7.01
1954	455.50	247.42	18.41	17.95	8.01	3.59
1955	545.40	263.48	20.70	22.19	9.81	7.81

TABLE I.11

COAL

Year	Value ($ million)	Quantity (millions of 1936 dollars)	F.O.B. price (1936 = 10)	Indirect price (1936 = 10)	Indirect price deflated by wholesale price index (1936 = 10)	Direct price (1936 = 10)	Direct price deflated by wholesale price index (1936 = 10)	Price of petroleum deflated by wholesale price index (1936 = 10)	Tariff rates (per cent)
1926	66.36	51.60	12.86	11.38	8.45	11.42	8.48	10.34	9.90
1927	66.56	53.50	12.44	11.15	8.48	11.62	8.84	9.57	9.63
1928	67.50	56.20	12.01	10.94	8.43	10.85	8.36	9.21	9.70
1929	65.60	56.94	11.52	10.71	8.32	10.91	8.48	9.08	10.45
1930	62.33	55.21	11.29	10.54	9.04	10.77	9.24	10.03	10.54
1931	40.55	39.10	10.37	10.40	10.71	10.62	10.94	11.04	18.74
1932	34.50	37.10	9.30	9.87	10.99	10.39	11.57	11.35	20.58
1933	30.89	34.59	8.93	9.57	10.60	9.99	11.06	11.53	23.57
1934	39.83	41.15	9.68	9.72	10.07	10.28	10.65	11.02	19.00
1935	36.95	37.70	9.80	9.92	10.17	10.29	10.55	10.54	21.08
1936	38.64	38.64	10.00	10.00	10.00	10.00	10.00	10.00	21.81
1937	40.90	40.61	10.07	9.91	8.90	10.06	9.04	9.26	22.78
1938	38.00	36.82	10.32	10.24	9.72	10.35	9.82	9.64	22.29
1939	44.53	44.09	10.10	10.05	9.80	10.38	10.13	9.51	21.78
1946	130.04	69.81	18.68			12.61			13.74
1947	147.70	72.87	20.27	15.45	9.16	13.88	8.23	7.58	13.52
1948	197.00	79.18	24.88	17.84	8.93	15.78	7.90	7.85	6.44
1949	149.50	57.72	25.90	18.66	9.11	16.42	8.01	7.88	5.85
1950	182.80	67.04	26.82	18.92	8.67	17.15	7.86	7.77	4.67
1951	179.80	67.42	26.67	19.34	7.80	17.61	7.10	6.71	5.00
1952	160.60	63.55	25.27	18.66	7.99	17.99	7.70	7.02	4.92
1953	144.20	55.89	25.80	19.15	8.40	18.21	7.99	7.32	5.07
1954	110.50	48.06	23.93	18.01	8.03	17.66	7.88	7.56	5.30
1955	113.70	48.88	23.26	17.44	7.71	17.58	7.78	7.41	5.08

TABLE I.12

PETROLEUM AND PETROLEUM PRODUCTS

Year	Value ($ million)	Quantity (millions of 1936 dollars)	F.O.B. price (1936 = 10)	Indirect price (1936 = 10)	Indirect price deflated by wholesale price index (1936 = 10)	Direct price (1936 = 10)	Direct price deflated by wholesale price index (1936 = 10)	Price of coal deflated by wholesale price index (1936 = 10)	Tariff rates (per cent)
1926	52.51	32.35	16.23	14.51	10.78	13.39	9.95	8.48	3.10
1927	53.84	37.91	14.20	13.24	10.07	11.24	8.55	8.84	3.07
1928	62.63	47.23	13.26	13.38	9.54	10.96	8.44	8.36	2.82
1929	77.84	56.86	13.69	12.75	9.91	11.07	8.60	8.48	2.65
1930	66.62	52.50	12.69	11.33	9.72	10.75	9.22	9.24	3.72
1931	40.63	47.63	8.53	9.00	9.27	8.85	9.11	10.94	7.80
1932	43.47	42.58	10.21	9.57	10.66	10.33	11.50	11.57	6.74
1933	31.05	39.81	7.80	8.16	9.04	9.24	10.23	11.06	5.31
1934	41.33	42.70	9.68	9.52	9.87	9.92	10.28	10.65	3.15
1935	44.09	46.56	9.47	9.35	9.59	9.91	10.16	10.55	3.15
1936	49.73	49.73	10.00	10.00	10.00	10.00	10.00	10.00	2.39
1937	59.01	54.89	10.75	12.06	10.84	10.20	9.16	9.04	2.08
1938	55.61	54.10	10.28	10.55	10.01	10.08	9.56	9.82	2.86
1939	55.91	57.64	9.70	10.03	9.79	9.77	9.53	10.13	3.32
1946	123.74	98.21	12.60						2.92
1947	207.20	129.26	16.03	23.05	13.66	13.88	8.23	8.23	3.46
1948	301.80	141.56	21.32	24.35	12.19	17.52	8.77	7.90	2.38
1949	274.60	127.48	21.54	22.28	10.87	18.29	8.93	8.01	1.86
1950	307.90	142.94	21.54	21.01	9.63	19.28	8.84	7.86	1.89
1951	353.90	153.80	23.01	28.16	11.35	18.65	7.52	7.10	1.94
1952	341.90	160.67	21.28	22.17	9.49	18.07	7.74	7.70	2.19
1953	358.00	162.65	22.01	21.16	9.28	18.58	8.15	7.99	2.25
1954	345.00	156.82	22.00	21.60	9.63	18.99	8.47	7.88	2.03
1955	373.60	172.80	21.62	24.39	10.79	18.86	8.34	7.78	2.11

TABLE I.13

FUELS

Year	Value ($ million)	Quantity (millions of 1936 dollars)	F.O.B. price (1936 = 10)	Indirect price (1936 = 10)	Direct price (1936 = 10)	Direct price deflated by wholesale price index (1936 = 10)	Tariff rates (per cent)
1926	118.52	80.40	14.74	13.51	12.76	9.48	6.92
1927	119.45	89.08	13.41	12.57	11.36	8.64	6.76
1928	130.22	102.70	12.68	11.92	10.92	8.41	6.39
1929	140.69	110.60	12.72	12.10	11.02	8.56	6.35
1930	128.39	106.46	12.06	11.08	10.76	9.23	7.04
1931	80.79	86.50	9.34	9.45	9.42	9.70	13.34
1932	77.93	79.60	9.79	9.67	10.35	11.53	12.87
1933	61.96	74.83	8.28	8.61	9.48	10.50	14.41
1934	81.17	84.03	9.66	9.58	10.04	10.40	10.93
1935	81.04	84.50	9.59	9.53	10.03	10.29	11.31
1936	88.38	88.38	10.00	10.00	10.00	10.00	10.87
1937	100.14	96.01	10.43	11.37	10.16	9.12	10.53
1938	93.78	92.94	10.30	10.45	10.17	9.65	8.43
1939	100.38	101.81	9.86	10.04	9.96	9.72	11.51
1946	253.52	167.34	15.15		12.01		8.48
1947	354.70	198.71	17.85	23.05	13.88	8.23	7.66
1948	498.50	217.88	22.88	24.35	16.96	8.49	3.98
1949	425.40	183.52	23.18	22.28	17.69	8.63	3.30
1950	491.40	206.48	23.80	21.00	18.60	8.52	2.94
1951	534.30	217.02	24.62	28.16	18.32	7.38	2.99
1952	503.90	218.90	23.02	22.17	18.04	7.73	2.99
1953	503.60	212.67	23.68	21.16	18.46	8.10	3.08
1954	457.80	199.83	22.91	21.60	18.56	8.28	2.85
1955	489.90	218.41	22.43	24.39	18.45	8.16	2.85

TABLE I.14

BASIC CHEMICALS

Year	Value ($ million)	Direct price (1936=10)	Tariff rates (per cent)
1926	17.99	11.15	7.89
1927	19.07	10.39	7.66
1928	21.00	10.15	7.61
1929	23.70	10.29	7.42
1930	22.62	10.09	7.47
1931	19.26	9.96	9.91
1932	16.81	10.51	10.65
1933	13.80	10.33	12.25
1934	26.57	10.42	6.81
1935	17.04	10.38	10.68
1936	17.87	10.00	9.96
1937	22.10	10.20	8.64
1938	22.80	10.14	8.20
1939	27.71	9.68	7.90
1946	63.30	10.38	9.71
1947	74.20	11.40	9.11
1948	79.30	12.41	9.28
1949	90.80	12.95	10.19
1950	107.20	13.70	8.69
1951	135.40	15.22	8.35
1952	137.20	14.96	8.11
1953	164.80	15.14	8.54
1954	162.10	14.72	8.88
1955	197.10	14.63	7.34

TABLE I.15

MISCELLANEOUS INVESTMENT GOODS

Year	Value ($ million)	Tariff rates (per cent)
1926	3.74	9.63
1927	3.99	10.03
1928	10.35	4.73
1929	15.19	3.42
1930	3.31	12.38
1931	2.01	13.96
1932	1.26	14.28
1933	1.05	13.33
1934	1.60	14.37
1935	1.73	9.82
1936	1.99	10.05
1937	3.07	9.44
1938	2.03	11.33
1939	2.14	11.21
1946	6.14	18.89
1947	10.50	17.90
1948	12.50	13.68
1949	11.25	13.24
1950	9.96	11.94
1951	17.20	10.63
1952	17.47	11.73
1953	23.79	8.02
1954	15.04	13.76
1955	21.40	14.00

APPENDIXES

TABLE I.16

AIRCRAFT AND PARTS

Year	Value ($ million)	Tariff rates (per cent)
1926	.20	20.00
1927	.90	20.00
1928	2.70	17.03
1929	3.30	17.57
1930	1.80	20.55
1931	.70	24.28
1932	.40	20.00
1933	.10	50.00
1934	.30	33.33
1935	2.60	3.46
1936	4.40	4.31
1937	2.60	19.23
1938	4.70	11.98
1939	8.10	8.77
1946	11.90	9.57
1947	18.20	8.46
1948	13.00	5.54
1949	22.90	4.85
1950	18.80	7.18
1951	61.10	10.37
1952	162.60	3.67
1953	158.10	.35
1954	115.30	.22
1955	171.70	.73

TABLE I.17

SPECIAL ITEMS

Year	Value ($ million)	Tariff rates (per cent)
1926	6.20	2.90
1927	9.57	1.78
1928	7.16	2.37
1929	8.86	1.57
1930	8.03	1.74
1931	5.59	3.04
1932	5.41	2.03
1933	3.88	3.87
1934	4.04	3.63
1935	4.39	4.10
1936	5.05	3.16
1937	3.55	5.07
1938	3.11	5.19
1939	4.79	3.34
1946	8.73	4.35
1947	6.87	5.13
1948	6.02	3.82
1949	7.62	5.11
1950	6.09	8.04
1951	14.30	4.41
1952	25.11	2.23
1953	36.41	1.18
1954	32.74	2.38
1955	55.30	1.34

TABLE I.18

TOTAL IMPORTS

Year	Value of total imports ($ million)	Value of those imports represented in the F.O.B. price index ($ million)	Quantity (value in 1936 dollars of imports represented in price index)	F.O.B. price (1936 = 10)	Indirect price (1936 = 10)
1926	988.80	960.67	656.65	14.63	13.40
1927	1057.40	1023.87	735.54	13.92	12.49
1928	1192.20	1150.99	839.53	13.71	12.09
1929	1267.60	1216.54	913.32	13.32	11.79
1930	980.40	944.64	812.94	11.62	10.68
1931	608.40	580.84	593.91	9.78	9.61
1932	440.00	416.12	434.82	9.57	9.68
1933	391.70	372.87	407.95	9.14	9.57
1934	501.90	469.39	481.92	9.74	9.86
1935	544.30	518.54	530.51	9.78	9.74
1936	632.90	603.59	603.59	10.00	10.00
1937	806.70	775.38	706.82	10.97	10.91
1938	674.70	642.06	630.09	10.19	10.07
1939	738.70	695.96	682.98	10.19	10.27
1946	1859.10	1769.03	1072.79	16.49	
1947	2566.70	2456.93	1295.85	18.96	17.95
1948	2628.90	2518.08	1168.48	21.55	19.06
1949	2755.30	2622.73	1186.22	22.11	19.35
1950	3167.60	3025.55	1272.84	23.77	20.72
1951	4077.50	3849.50	1415.26	27.20	24.99
1952	4025.10	3682.72	1548.01	23.79	21.53
1953	4375.80	3992.70	1693.26	23.58	21.06
1954	4083.50	3758.32	1592.51	23.60	21.28
1955	4708.90	4264.40	1791.76	23.80	21.94

Year	Indirect price deflated by wholesale price index (1936 = 10)	Published DBS import price index (1936 = 10)	Tariff rates on total imports (per cent)	Tariff rates on imports represented in price index (per cent)
1926	9.96	14.64	15.64	15.89
1927	9.50	13.87	15.86	16.16
1928	9.31	13.59	16.20	16.54
1929	9.16	13.26	15.58	15.98
1930	9.16	11.97	16.04	16.37
1931	9.90	10.01	19.45	19.93
1932	10.79	9.85	18.25	18.76
1933	10.60	9.45	18.17	18.54
1934	10.11	10.15	16.01	16.63
1935	9.99	9.83	14.90	15.21
1936	10.00	10.00	13.95	14.24
1937	9.80	10.98	12.32	12.45
1938	9.55	10.15	13.44	13.69
1939	10.02	10.18	13.05	13.38
1946			11.29	
1947	10.64	19.37	11.73	11.82
1948	9.54	21.88	8.36	8.33
1949	9.44	22.58	8.20	7.77
1950	9.50	24.14	7.96	7.93
1951	10.07	27.62	8.36	8.33
1952	9.22	24.16	8.78	9.06
1953	9.24	23.94	9.32	9.79
1954	9.49	23.96	9.44	9.79
1955	9.70	24.18	9.39	10.08

TABLE I.19

MISCELLANEOUS SERIES

Year	Disposable personal income in 1936 dollars, deflated by population (in $10)	Gross national product in 1949 dollars (in $00,000,000)
1926	34.41	75.76
1927	36.09	82.70
1928	37.74	90.37
1929	36.87	90.61
1930	34.13	86.79
1931	31.48	75.67
1932	28.37	67.98
1933	27.12	63.59
1934	29.50	71.27
1935	30.99	76.78
1936	31.80	80.22
1937	34.51	88.20
1938	34.17	88.71
1939	36.12	95.36
1947	55.10	154.46
1948	54.62	157.35
1949	54.37	163.43
1950	54.89	174.71
1951	56.24	185.47
1952	57.63	200.27
1953	59.52	207.94
1954	57.68	201.86
1955	60.89	219.61

Year	Disposable personal income ($ tens of millions)	Time trend	Consumer price index (1936 = 10)
1926	404	1	12.42
1927	425	2	12.21
1928	456	3	12.27
1929	459	4	12.41
1930	429	5	12.32
1931	363	6	11.11
1932	300	7	10.10
1933	277	8	9.62
1934	309	9	9.75
1935	329	10	9.80
1936	348	11	10.00
1937	393	12	10.31
1938	398	13	10.43
1939	421	14	10.34
1947	960	22	13.88
1948	1112	23	15.88
1949	1197	24	16.37
1950	1267	25	16.84
1951	1466	26	18.61
1952	1589	27	19.07
1953	1670	28	18.90
1954	1679	29	19.02
1955	1820	30	19.05

ALTERNATIVE CLASSIFICATIONS OF
CANADIAN IMPORTS

THE PRINCIPAL DBS classification of Canadian imports is the "commodity component" classification, published in *Trade of Canada*. Imports are divided into nine groups which in turn contain more than one hundred subgroups. The main groups are: agricultural and vegetable products; animals and animal products; fibres, textiles, and textile products; wood and wood products; iron and steel products; non-ferrous metals and products; non-metallic minerals and products; chemicals and fertilizers; and miscellaneous. This classification is cross-classified by country of origin. Price series exist for most groups. An "animal–vegetable–mineral" classification of this kind, however, is not well suited to our purposes since the members of a group may have quite unrelated end uses and, therefore, be subject to quite different laws of demand.

DBS also publishes the "Brussels" classification of imports into raw materials, partly manufactured commodities, and fully manufactured commodities. But, for our purposes, it is doubtful whether this is an improvement on the commodity component classification.

A third DBS classification is into imports of farm origin, wildlife origin, sea origin, mineral origin, forest origin, and mixed origin. This is perhaps the least useful classification from our point of view.

The last of the official classifications is the most useful: producers' materials (building and construction materials, manufacturers' materials, other); producers' equipment; fuel, electricity, and lubricants; transportation equipment; auxiliary materials for commerce and industry (advertising materials and containers); consumer goods. But there were certain difficulties with the classification and it was discontinued after 1939.

In addition to the official DBS classifications, there are available two classifications published quarterly by the Bank of Canada in its monthly *Statistical Summary* and two classifications published by David Slater in *Canada's Imports* (Ottawa, 1957).

The first of the two Bank of Canada classifications differs only in minor details from the DBS commodity component classification. It was discontinued in 1956. The second Bank of Canada classification is a slightly modified version of the Standard International Trade Classification into fuels and lubricants, crude and semi-manufactured industrial materials, investment goods, and consumer goods. The last three groups are subdivided into four, four, and five subgroups, respectively. Thus industrial materials are subdivided into textile, leather and fur materials; metal materials; chemical materials; and other industrial materials. Investment goods are subdivided into machinery and parts; electrical machinery; aircraft, other transport equipment and parts; and construction materials, structural steel and pipe. Finally the consumer goods category is subdivided into food, beverages and tobacco; clothing, household textiles and leather goods; passenger automobiles: engines, parts, and finished vehicles; household durables and semi-durables; and other manufactured goods. The series are available on a quarterly basis. Of those considered so far, this classification is best suited to our needs. The value series suffer, however, from two major drawbacks—they extend back only to 1950, and there are no corresponding price series.

The first of Slater's classifications is a minor modification of the first Bank of Canada classification. Both Slater's and the Bank of Canada's classifications are regroupings of the basic *Trade of Canada* subgroups. The objective was a classification into groups whose elements would be more homogeneous in end use than is the case with the DBS commodity component classification. Series based on this regrouping have the considerable advantage that they can easily be constructed from published sources. They suffer, however, from the disadvantage that they are based on the *Trade of Canada* subgroups rather than on the individual items of *Trade of Canada*. The subgroups already involve a considerable aggregation of items which, from our point of view, may be quite heterogeneous. Recognizing this difficulty, Slater constructed a second classification based on the individual items. This classification is described in the text.

THE CONSTRUCTION OF THE
INDIRECT PRICE INDICES

THE INDIRECT PRICE INDICES were derived from the f.o.b. indices by correcting separately for freight, tariffs, and commodity taxes. The three phases of the correction procedure are described in this appendix. The following symbolism is employed:

p''' = the Laspeyres f.o.b. price index for a particular category of imports
p'' = the f.o.b. price index corrected for freight only
p' = the f.o.b. price index corrected for freight and tariffs
p = the indirect price index
T = the average *ad valorem* rate of duty on a particular category of imports
T' = the average rate of commodity tax levied on a particular category of imports
x = the quantity of a particular commodity imported
p = the f.o.b. price of a particular imported commodity
t = the *ad valorem* rate of duty on a particular commodity
f = the freight per unit of quantity, for an individual commodity
Z = the ratio of the total freight bill to the total f.o.b. value of imports
F = the over-all index of freight rates
F_r = the index of rail freight rates
F_s = the index of ocean freight rates
α = the ratio of ocean freight to rail freight

The subscript "0" refers to the quantity to the base year.

TAXES[1]

Let us consider the final step first. The correction of P' for commodity taxes was achieved by means of the formula

(III.1)
$$P - P'\left(\frac{1 + T'}{1 + T_0'}\right)$$

which presupposes the existence of a series of average commodity taxes.

Imports are subject to the regular federal, provincial, and municipal commodity taxes. Municipal sales taxes are important in Montreal and Quebec City, but taking the whole country in purview, are insignificant and are ignored. The federal government levies, or has levied at some time during the period under review, a retail sales tax, a special excise tax, and a retail purchase tax. The latter, which was first imposed in 1942 and abandoned in 1949, was levied on a limited range of commodities, does not seem to have been of great importance for any of our categories, and is ignored. The federal sales tax is levied on most goods sold at retail; conspicuous exemptions are most dairy products, most raw and unprepared foods, sugar, coal, petroleum, building materials (after 1938), machinery and equipment for manufacturing industries (after 1945). The federal excise tax is levied on a limited range of goods, the principal being automobiles, electrical appliances (including radios and phonographs), cigarettes and wine. In addition to the regular excise tax, the federal government imposed, in the 'thirties, a special excise tax on imports.[2] Alberta in 1936 imposed the first provincial sales tax, and most provinces have followed suit. The following commodities are universally exempted: foodstuffs, drugs, farming and fishing implements, gasoline, coal. Finally, provincial excise taxes are levied on gasoline destined for highway use and on alcoholic beverages.

Two of the import categories, food and raw materials and coal, appear to have been substantially exempt from all commodity taxes throughout the period considered. It is assumed that they were entirely exempt. The average rates applied to other categories are set out in Table III.1. Each entry in Table III.1

TABLE III.1

COMMODITY TAX RATES, T'

	Beverages and tobacco			Clothing and textiles, etc.			Furniture, household appliances, etc.			
Year	Federal Sales Tax	Federal Excise Tax	Total	Federal Sales Tax	Provincial Sales Tax	Total	Federal Sales Tax	Federal Excise Tax	Provincial Sales Tax	Total
1926	5.0	1.0	6.0	5.0	0.0	5.0	5.0	0.0	0.0	5.0
1927	4.0	1.0	5.0	4.0	0.0	4.0	4.0	0.0	0.0	4.0
1928	3.0	1.0	4.0	3.0	0.0	3.0	3.0	0.0	0.0	3.0
1929	2.2	1.0	3.2	2.2	0.0	2.2	2.2	0.0	0.0	2.2
1930	1.2	1.0	3.2	1.2	0.0	1.2	1.2	0.0	0.0	1.2
1931	2.5	1.0	3.5	2.5	0.0	2.5	2.5	0.0	0.0	2.5
1932	5.3	1.0	6.3	5.3	0.0	5.3	5.3	0.0	0.0	5.3
1933	6.0	1.0	7.0	6.0	0.0	6.0	6.0	0.0	0.0	6.0
1934	6.0	1.0	7.0	6.0	0.0	6.0	6.0	0.0	0.0	6.0
1935	6.0	1.0	7.0	6.0	0.0	6.0	6.0	0.0	0.0	6.0
1936	7.3	1.0	8.3	7.3	0.1	7.4	7.3	0.0	0.1	7.4
1937	8.0	1.0	9.0	8.0	0.1	8.1	8.0	0.0	0.1	8.1
1938	8.0	1.0	9.0	8.0	0.1	8.1	8.0	0.0	0.1	8.1
1939	8.0	1.0	9.0	8.0	0.1	8.1	8.0	0.0	0.1	8.1
1946	8.0	5.0	13.0	8.0	0.7	8.7	8.0	0.2	0.7	8.9
1947	8.0	5.0	13.0	8.0	0.7	8.7	8.0	2.5	0.7	11.2
1948	8.0	5.0	13.0	8.0	0.8	8.8	8.0	11.3	0.8	20.1
1949	8.0	5.0	13.0	8.0	0.8	8.8	8.0	0.0	0.8	8.8
1950	8.0	5.0	13.0	8.0	0.9	8.9	8.0	0.0	0.9	8.9
1951	9.5	4.0	13.5	9.5	1.0	10.5	9.5	9.2	1.0	19.7
1952	10.0	4.0	14.0	10.0	1.0	11.0	10.0	4.6	1.0	15.6
1953	10.0	4.0	14.0	10.0	1.0	11.0	10.0	0.2	1.0	11.2
1954	10.0	4.0	14.0	10.0	1.0	11.0	10.0	0.2	1.0	11.2
1955	10.0	4.0	14.0	10.0	1.0	11.0	10.0	0.2	1.0	11.2

was obtained by multiplying the tax rate in the year in question by the ratio to the total f.o.b. value of the category, in 1928, 1938, and 1954, of the total value of those elements which were subject to tax. This method imparts a downward bias to the average rate of tax since the f.o.b. value of taxed imports will be depressed by the tax-inflated prices.

TABLE III.1 (*continued*)

Year	Consumer goods			Automobiles				Machinery and equipment		
	Federal Sales Tax	Provincial Sales Tax	Total	Federal Sales Tax	Federal Excise Tax	Provincial Sales Tax	Total	Federal Sales Tax	Provincial Sales Tax	Total
1926	5.0		5.0	5.0			5.0	5.0		5.0
1927	4.0		4.0	4.0			4.0	4.0		4.0
1928	3.0		3.0	3.0			3.0	3.0		3.0
1929	2.2		2.2	2.2			2.2	2.2		2.2
1930	1.2		1.2	1.2			1.2	1.2		1.2
1931	2.5		2.5	2.5			2.5	2.5		2.5
1932	5.3		5.3	5.3			5.3	5.3		5.3
1933	6.0		6.0	6.0			6.0	6.0		6.0
1934	6.0		6.0	6.0			6.0	6.0		6.0
1935	6.0		6.0	6.0			6.0	6.0		6.0
1936	7.3	0.1	7.4	7.3	2.0	0.1	9.4	7.3		7.3
1937	8.0	0.1	8.1	8.0	2.0	0.1	10.1	8.0		8.0
1938	8.0	0.1	8.1	8.0	2.0	0.1	10.1	8.0		8.0
1939	8.0	0.1	8.1	8.0	2.0	0.1	10.1	8.0		8.0
1946	8.0	0.7	8.7	8.0	10.0	0.7	18.7	1.6	0.1	1.7
1947	8.0	0.7	8.7	8.0	11.0	0.7	19.7	1.6	0.1	1.7
1948	8.0	0.8	8.8	8.0	22.0	0.8	30.8	1.6	0.2	1.8
1949	8.0	0.8	8.8	8.0	10.0	0.8	18.8	1.6	0.2	1.8
1950	8.0	0.9	8.9	8.0	11.2	0.9	20.1	1.6	0.2	1.8
1951	9.5	1.0	10.5	9.5	22.5	1.0	33.0	1.9	0.2	2.1
1952	10.0	1.0	11.0	10.0	17.5	1.0	28.5	2.0	0.2	2.2
1953	10.0	1.0	11.0	10.0	15.0	1.0	26.0	2.0	0.2	2.2
1954	10.0	1.0	11.0	10.0	15.0	1.0	26.0	2.0	0.2	2.2
1955	10.0	1.0	11.0	10.0	15.0	1.0	26.0	2.0	0.2	2.2

Year	Materials for investment in structures Federal Sales Tax—Total	Petroleum Provincial Excise Tax*—Total	Unassigned industrial materials Federal Sales Tax—Total
1926	5.0	3.0	5.0
1927	4.0	3.0	4.0
1928	3.0	3.0	3.0
1929	2.2	5.0	2.2
1930	1.2	5.0	1.2
1931	2.5	5.0	2.5
1932	5.3	6.0	5.3
1933	6.0	6.0	6.0
1934	6.0	6.0	6.0
1935	6.0	6.0	6.0
1936	7.3	6.0	7.3
1937	8.0	6.0	8.0
1938	4.0	6.0	8.0
1939		7.0	8.0
1946		11.0	8.0
1947		11.0	8.0
1948		11.0	8.0
1949		11.0	8.0
1950		11.0	8.0
1951		11.5	9.5
1952		11.5	10.0
1953		11.5	10.0
1954		11.5	10.0
1955		11.5	10.0

*Includes wartime federal excise tax of 3 per cent in 1946 and 1947.

DUTIES

Let us consider now the problem of deriving P' from P'', that is, of adjusting P'' for import duties. By definition

$$(III.2) \qquad P' = \frac{\sum x_0[p(1 + t) + f]}{\sum x_0[p_0(1 + t_0) + f_0]}.$$

Elementary developments of (III.2) give

$$(III.3) \qquad P' = \left[(1 + Z_0)P'' + T_0\left(\frac{\sum x_0 pt}{\sum x_0 p_0 t}\right)\right] \Big/ [1 + Z_0 + T_0]$$

$\sum x_0 pt / \sum x_0 p_0 t_0$ is the ratio to duty collected in the base period of the duty which would have been collected in the period under consideration if the base period quantities had been imported. It is estimated by $P'''(T/T_0)$. Substituting this estimator in (III.3)

$$(III.4) \qquad P' = [(1 + Z_0)P'' + TP''']/[1 + Z_0 + T_0].$$

In cases where transportation costs are a small part of landed value, (III.4) may be approximated by

$$(III.5) \qquad P' = [P'' + TP''']/[1 + T_0].$$

In the cases of coal, petroleum and petroleum products, and fuels, where transportation costs represent a substantial part of total costs, such an approximation is clearly inadmissible. In those cases formula (III.4) was retained. In all other cases, formula (III.5) was used.

FREIGHT

There remains the problem of estimating P'', that is, of correcting P''' for freight. The formula used is

$$(III.6) \qquad P'' = (P''' + Z_0 F)/(1 + Z_0)$$

which presupposes the existence, for each category, of a reliable index of freight rates.

There are no published freight indices for Canadian imports. And the materials from which indices might be constructed are scant and highly aggregative. The exception to the rule is coal, for which more detailed information is available and which will be accorded special treatment later. In the meantime, expressions such as "the value of total imports" and "the total freight bill" must be interpreted as net of coal.

The method by which an index of freights was constructed is based on the twin assumptions that imports enter either by rail or by sea, and that imports from the United States are carried by rail while imports from other countries are carried by sea.[3] The fundamental formula is

$$F = (F_r + \alpha_0 F_s)/(1 + \alpha_0).$$

TABLE III.2

VALUES OF k

Food and food materials	3.24
Beverages and tobacco	17.16
Clothing and textiles, etc.	4.64
Furniture, household appliances, etc.	1.08
Miscellaneous consumer goods	1.60
Automobiles, trucks, and parts	0.08
Machinery and equipment	0.88
Materials for investment in structures	1.36
Unassigned industrial materials	1.68

The only available information about α refers to the year 1936 and to total imports. In that year α was approximately 2.[4] It would be unreasonable, however, to apply $\alpha = 2$ to every category of imports. Accordingly, in the case of all categories but petroleum, it was multiplied by the "correction factor"

$$k = \frac{\left(\dfrac{\text{value of imports of the type considered from the rest of the world}}{\text{value of imports of the type considered from the United States}}\right) \div}{\left(\dfrac{\text{value of total imports from the rest of the world}}{\text{value of total imports from the United States}}\right)}$$

TABLE III.3

FREIGHT RATE INDICES (1936 = 100)

Year	Index of ocean freight rates	Index of United States rail freight rates
1926	130.6	111.0
1927	129.8	110.9
1928	120.5	111.0
1929	116.6	110.5
1930	87.5	108.9
1931	88.1	107.9
1932	70.5	107.2
1933	78.6	102.3
1934	88.9	100.4
1935	88.2	101.6
1936	100.0	100.0
1937	155.0	95.9
1938	111.6	100.9
1938 (Jan.–Aug.)	114.0	
1939		99.8
1939 (Jan.–Aug.)	102.1	
1947	369.9*	110.4
1948	301.6	128.3
1949	231.5	137.3
1950	191.0	136.3
1951	383.6	137.0
1952	225.9	146.7
1953	177.7	151.6
1954	194.7	145.7
1955	290.8	140.6

*Obtained by linking the *Economist* index, which was not published from August 1939 to January 1948, with the tramp freight index published by *Norwegian Shipping News*.

APPENDIXES

TABLE III.4

FINAL FREIGHT INDICES

Year	Food and food materials	Beverages and tobacco	Clothing and textiles, etc.	Furniture, household appliances, etc.	Miscellaneous consumer goods	Automobiles, trucks, and parts
1926	126.0	129.5	127.1	121.2	123.1	112.5
1927	125.4	128.8	126.5	120.8	122.6	112.4
1928	118.3	120.0	118.8	115.9	116.8	111.7
1929	115.2	116.3	115.5	113.7	114.3	111.0
1930	92.5	88.7	91.3	97.8	95.7	107.3
1931	92.8	89.2	91.6	97.6	95.7	106.4
1932	79.2	72.5	77.0	88.1	84.6	104.5
1933	84.2	79.9	82.8	90.0	87.7	100.5
1934	91.6	89.5	90.9	94.4	93.3	99.5
1935	91.4	88.9	90.6	94.6	93.4	100.6
1936	100.0	100.0	100.0	100.0	100.0	100.0
1937	141.1	151.8	144.5	126.6	132.2	99.5
1938	109.1	111.0	109.7	106.4	107.5	101.7
1939	101.6	102.0	101.7	101.0	101.2	100.0
1947	308.7	355.7	323.9	245.1	270.0	129.6
1948	260.7	292.1	270.9	218.3	234.9	141.1
1949	209.3	226.3	214.8	186.2	195.3	144.2
1950	178.1	188.0	181.3	164.7	170.0	140.3
1951	325.4	363.2	339.3	265.0	288.8	155.3
1952	207.2	221.5	211.9	187.8	195.4	152.5
1953	171.5	168.7	173.1	165.1	167.7	153.5
1954	183.1	192.6	186.0	171.1	175.8	149.3
1955	255.4	282.5	264.2	218.5	233.0	151.7

Year	Machinery and equipment	Materials for investment in structures	Coal	Petroleum and petroleum products	Unassigned industrial materials
1926	120.2	122.3	111.0	126.2	123.3
1927	119.8	121.8	110.9	125.6	122.8
1928	115.5	116.5	111.0	118.4	117.0
1929	113.4	114.0	110.5	115.2	114.3
1930	98.9	96.6	108.9	92.2	95.5
1931	98.6	96.5	107.9	92.5	95.5
1932	90.0	86.1	107.2	78.7	84.2
1933	91.2	88.6	102.3	83.9	87.4
1934	95.0	93.8	100.4	91.5	93.2
1935	95.3	82.7	101.6	91.2	93.2
1936	100.0	100.0	100.0	100.0	100.0
1937	123.6	130.0	95.9	141.8	132.9
1938	105.9	107.1	100.9	109.2	107.6
1939	100.9	101.1	99.8	101.6	191.2
1947	231.9	259.9	110.4	312.0	273.1
1948	209.4	228.2	128.3	262.9	236.9
1949	181.4	191.5	137.3	210.5	196.4
1950	161.9	167.8	136.3	178.8	170.6
1951	252.4	279.1	137.0	328.6	291.6
1952	183.8	192.3	146.7	208.2	196.3
1953	163.8	166.6	151.6	171.9	168.0
1954	168.6	173.9	145.7	183.8	176.4
1955	210.9	227.2	140.6	257.3	234.8

which was computed for the three years 1928, 1938, and 1954, and averaged. The final formula, then, was

$$F = (F_r + k\alpha_0 F_s)/(1 + k\alpha_0).$$

The series of ocean freight rates F and of rail freight rates F_r are set out in Table III.3. F_s was obtained by linking the present *Economist* index of tramp shipping freights to earlier indexes published on different base years, and adjusting for changes in the sterling–Canadian dollar exchange rate. The *Economist* index covers United Kingdom exports and imports *via* all shipping routes. F_r was obtained by computing the revenue per ton mile on United States Class I steam railways.[5]

The Special Case of Coal

Most imported coal comes from the United States. It is shipped by rail to Lake Erie or Lake Ontario and thence by ship to the Canadian port of entry. In 1936 the rail freight on imports from the United States represented 84 per cent of the total freight bill to the port of entry.[6] Accordingly, the index of United States rail freight rates has been adopted as the index of freight rates for coal.

The final freight indices are set out in Table III.4.

The indirect price index for aggregate imports was obtained by taking a weighted average of the indirect price indices of individual categories. The weights are proportional to the relative values of the base year.

ESTIMATION BIAS ARISING FROM
ERRORS OF OBSERVATION

IT IS SHOWN in this appendix that if measurements of the import price variable are subject to error the least squares estimates of the price coefficient, and hence the derived estimates of the price elasticity, will be biased. In particular, it is shown, under plausible assumptions, that if the same price variable appears both as independent variable and as deflator in the denominator of the dependent quantity variable, the large-sample estimates of price elasticities will be biased towards minus one; that, on the other hand, if two different price variables are used, the estimates will be biased towards zero. All the essentials of the problem, without irrelevant complications, appear in the special case in which price is the only explanatory variable:

(IV.1) $$X = \alpha_0 + \alpha_1 P + \epsilon_1.$$

But

(IV.2) $$X = \frac{V}{P}$$

where V is a value series; hence

(IV.3) $$\frac{V}{P} = \alpha_0 + \alpha_1 P + \epsilon_1.$$

Imagine that two estimates of P, say P' and P'', exist and that P' is employed as the deflator of V, P'' as the independent variable. P' may be identified with the f.o.b. and indirect price series, P'' with the direct price series. P' and P'' are subject to errors of measurement, ϵ' and ϵ'', respectively, which are assumed to be independent of ϵ_1.

(IV.4) $$P = P' - \epsilon' = P'' - \epsilon''.$$

The least squares estimate of α_1 is

$$\text{est. } \alpha_1 = \text{cov.}\left(\frac{V}{P'}, P''\right)$$

which, in the light of (IV.4) and for large samples, reduces to[1]

(IV.5) $$\text{est. } \alpha_1 = \left[E\left(V\frac{P + \epsilon''}{P + \epsilon'}\right) - E(P)E\left(\frac{V}{P + \epsilon'}\right)\right]$$
$$/[\text{var.}(P) + \text{var.}(\epsilon'') + 2\,\text{cov.}(P, \epsilon'')].$$

Progress in assessing the bias is conditional upon the evaluation of

$$E\left(V\frac{P + \epsilon''}{P + \epsilon'}\right) \quad \text{and} \quad E\left(\frac{V}{P + \epsilon'}\right).$$

To this end, consider the series expansions

(IV.6) $$(P + \epsilon')^{-1} = P^{-1}\left[1 - \left(\frac{\epsilon'}{P}\right) + \left(\frac{\epsilon'}{P}\right)^2 - \left(\frac{\epsilon'}{P}\right)^3 + \cdots\right]$$

and

(IV.7) $$P^{-1} = [E(P)]^{-1}\left\{1 - \left[\frac{p}{E(P)}\right] + \left[\frac{p}{E(P)}\right]^2 - \left[\frac{p}{E(P)}\right]^3 + \cdots\right\}$$

where

$$p = P - E(P)$$

is the deviation of P from its expectation. The series (IV.6) and (IV.7) converge absolutely if

$$\left|\frac{\epsilon'}{P}\right| \quad \text{and} \quad \left|\frac{p}{E(P)}\right|,$$

respectively, are less than unity. These conditions are assumed to be satisfied. Substituting from (IV.3), (IV.6), and (IV.7), ignoring terms of degree higher than three, and making use of Haldane's theorem again,[2] (IV.5) reduces to

(IV.8) $$\text{est. } \alpha_1 = \left\{-\alpha_0\left[\frac{\text{cov.}(P, \epsilon') + \text{cov.}(\epsilon', \epsilon'')}{E(P)}\right]\right.$$

$$\left. +\alpha_1[\text{var.}(P) + \text{cov.}(P, \epsilon'') - \text{cov.}(P, \epsilon') - \text{cov.}(\epsilon', \epsilon'')]\right\} \div$$

$$\{\text{var.}(P) + \text{var.}(\epsilon'') + 2\,\text{cov.}(P, \epsilon'')\}.$$

To a third degree approximation, therefore, the bias is

(IV.9) $$\text{est. } \alpha_1 - \alpha_1 = -\left\{\alpha_0\left[\frac{\text{cov.}(P, \epsilon') + \text{cov.}(\epsilon', \epsilon'')}{E(P)}\right]\right.$$

$$\left. +\alpha_1\left[\text{var.}(\epsilon'') + \text{cov.}(P, \epsilon') + \text{cov.}(P, \epsilon'') + \text{cov.}(\epsilon', \epsilon'')\right]\right\} \div$$

$$\{\text{var.}(P) + \text{var.}(\epsilon'') + 2\,\text{cov.}(P, \epsilon'')\}.$$

If the errors are independent of the true value of the price, this forbidding expression assumes the gentler form

(IV.10) $$\text{est. } \alpha_1 - \alpha_1 = -\left\{\left[\frac{\alpha_0 + \alpha_1 E(P)}{E(P)}\right]\text{cov.}(\epsilon', \epsilon'') + \alpha_1\,\text{var.}(\epsilon'')\right\}$$

$$/[\text{var.}(P) + \text{var.}(\epsilon'')].$$

Two cases merit special consideration.

Case 1. If $\text{cov.}(\epsilon', \epsilon'') = 0$, the bias reduces to

(IV.11) $$\text{est. } \alpha_1 - \alpha_1 = \frac{-\alpha_1\,\text{var.}(\epsilon'')}{\text{var.}(P) + \text{var.}(\epsilon'')}.$$

This expression is of sign opposite to that of α_1. If, as may be supposed, $\alpha_1 < 0$, the bias is positive, that is, the estimate of the price coefficient is biased towards zero. This is the case studied by Orcutt,[3] who implicitly assumed that $\epsilon' \equiv 0$ and, hence, that cov.$(\epsilon', \epsilon'') = 0$. It is also the case into which those estimates based on the direct price series fall. For it seems reasonable to suppose that errors in the measurement of P by the direct method are independent of errors in the f.o.b. series.

Case 2. If, on the other hand, the same price series is used as deflator and as independent variable, cov.$(\epsilon', \epsilon'') = $ var.(ϵ''). Hence

(IV.12)   est. $\alpha_1 - \alpha_1 = -\left[\dfrac{\alpha_0 + 2\alpha_1 E(P)}{E(P)}\right]\text{var.}(\epsilon'') \Big/ [\text{var.}(P) + \text{var.}(\epsilon'')]$.

The bias may be of either sign, or zero. It vanishes if

$$E(P) = -\tfrac{1}{2}\frac{\alpha_0}{\alpha_1},$$

that is, if the average price lies exactly half-way along the demand curve. If $E(P) > -\tfrac{1}{2}(\alpha_0/\alpha_1)$, that is, if the average price lies closer to the price inter-cept, the bias will be positive (est. α_1 will be biased towards zero). If the average price lies closer to the quantity intercept, the bias will be negative (est. α_1 will be biased away from zero).

Now the elasticity of a straight line demand curve is minus one at its mid-point; closer to the price intercept, the curve is elastic; and closer to the quantity intercept it is inelastic. In view of the conclusions set out above, one may con-jecture that the estimate of the demand *elasticity* is biased towards minus one. That this is indeed the case may easily be verified. The true elasticity of demand, at any assigned value of $E(P) = E(P') = E(P'')$, is, say,

$$\eta = \frac{\alpha_1 E(P)}{\alpha_0 + \alpha_1 P}$$

and the least squares estimate of the elasticity is

$$\text{est. } \eta = \frac{(\text{est. } \alpha_1)E(P)}{\text{est. } \alpha_0 + (\text{est. } \alpha_1)P}.$$

The denominator reduces to

$$\text{est. } \alpha_0 + (\text{est. } \alpha_1)P = \{\alpha_0 + \alpha_1 P\}\{1 + [E(P)]^{-2}\,\text{var.}(\epsilon'')\};$$

hence the estimation bias may be expressed as

(IV.13)   est. $\eta - \eta = \left\{\dfrac{E(P)}{\alpha_0 + \alpha_1 E(P)}\right\}\left\{\dfrac{\text{est. } \alpha_1}{1 + [E(P)]^{-2}\,\text{var.}(\epsilon'')} - \alpha_1\right\}.$

Now we know that the bias vanishes at the midpoint of the demand curve, where the elasticity is unity. Our conjecture is confirmed, therefore, if it can be shown that

(IV.14) $\dfrac{\partial}{\partial E(P)}\,(\text{est. } \eta - \eta) > 0.$

Evidently a sufficient condition for (IV.14) is

$$\frac{\partial(\text{est. } \alpha_1)}{\partial E(P)} > 0.$$

But, from (IV.12),

(IV.15) $$\frac{\partial(\text{est. } \alpha_1)}{\partial E(P)} = \frac{\alpha_1 \text{ var.}(\epsilon'')}{[E(P)]^2 [\text{var.}(P) + \text{var.}(\epsilon'')]} > 0.$$

A FORMAL TEST OF HOMOGENEITY[1]

IT IS CONVENIENT to adopt a notation which differs from that of chapters III and IV. The observations on the dependent variable y and on each of k independent variables $x_1, x_2, \ldots, x_k$ are assumed to be measured from the means of the variables and to be $(m + n)$ in number, m occurring in the first of the two subperiods and n in the other. Let x_k be the shift variable described in chapter III, section C. The observations may then be set out in matrix notation as follows:

$$\mathbf{y} = \begin{bmatrix} \mathbf{y}_1 \\ \mathbf{y}_2 \end{bmatrix} = \begin{bmatrix} y_1 \\ \vdots \\ y_m \\ \hline y_{m+1} \\ \vdots \\ y_{m+n} \end{bmatrix}$$

$$\mathbf{X} = \begin{bmatrix} \mathbf{X}_1 | \mathbf{O} \\ \hline \mathbf{X}_2 \end{bmatrix} = \begin{bmatrix} x_{11} & \cdots & x_{1,k-1} & | & 0 \\ \vdots & & \vdots & | & \vdots \\ x_{m1} & \cdots & x_{m,k-1} & | & 0 \\ \hline x_{m+1,1} & \cdots & x_{m+1,k-1} & & x_{m+1,k} \\ \vdots & & \vdots & & \vdots \\ x_{m+n,1} & \cdots & x_{m+n,k-1} & & x_{m+n,k} \end{bmatrix}.$$

The solid lines indicate partitioning. It is assumed that $m \geqslant (k - 1)$ and $n \geqslant k$ and that the ranks of $\mathbf{X}_1$ and $\mathbf{X}_2$ are $(k - 1)$ and k, respectively.

The problem is to test the hypothesis that no break in structure has occurred between the mth and $(m + 1)$th periods against the alternative hypothesis that a break has occurred. Denote the regression coefficients by

$$\overset{*}{\beta} = \begin{bmatrix} \beta_1 \\ \beta_2 \\ \vdots \\ \beta_{k-1} \end{bmatrix}, \quad \beta = \begin{bmatrix} \beta_1 \\ \beta_2 \\ \vdots \\ \beta_k \end{bmatrix} = \begin{bmatrix} \overset{*}{\beta} \\ \beta_k \end{bmatrix}, \quad \beta_1 = \begin{bmatrix} \beta_{11} \\ \beta_{21} \\ \vdots \\ \beta_{k-1,1} \end{bmatrix}, \quad \beta_2 = \begin{bmatrix} \beta_{12} \\ \beta_{22} \\ \vdots \\ \beta_{k2} \end{bmatrix}$$

where the matrix subscripts refer to the two subperiods. Then the null hypothesis and its alternative may be written

$$H_0 : \mathbf{y} = \mathbf{X}\beta + \varepsilon$$

$$H_a : \begin{matrix} \mathbf{y}_1 = \mathbf{X}_1\beta_1 + \varepsilon_1 \\ \mathbf{y}_2 = \mathbf{X}_2\beta_2 + \varepsilon_2 \end{matrix} \quad \text{or} \quad \begin{bmatrix} \mathbf{y}_1 \\ \mathbf{y}_2 \end{bmatrix} = \begin{bmatrix} \mathbf{X}_1 | \mathbf{O} \\ \mathbf{O} | \mathbf{X}_2 \end{bmatrix} \begin{bmatrix} \beta_1 \\ \beta_2 \end{bmatrix} + \begin{bmatrix} \varepsilon_1 \\ \varepsilon_2 \end{bmatrix}$$

where ε, ε_1, and ε_2 are $(m + n)$-, m-, and n-dimensional vectors of errors which are assumed to have zero means and constant variance σ^2 and to be distributed independently of the x's.

Denote by $\tilde{\beta}$, $\tilde{\beta}^*$, $\tilde{\beta}_1$, and $\tilde{\beta}_2$ the least squares estimates of β, β^*, β_1, and β_2 respectively. Then[2]

(V.1a)
$$\tilde{\beta} = (X_1'X_1)^{-1} \cdot X'y_1 = \begin{bmatrix} \tilde{\beta}^* \\ \tilde{\beta}_k \end{bmatrix}$$

(V.1b)
$$\tilde{\beta}_1 = (X_1'X_1)^{-1} \cdot X_1'y_1$$

(V.1c)
$$\tilde{\beta}_2 = (X_2'X_2)^{-1} \cdot X_2'y_2.$$

Under H_0, the sum of the squared residuals is

$$(y - X\tilde{\beta})'(y - X\tilde{\beta}) = \left\{ \begin{bmatrix} y_1 \\ y_2 \end{bmatrix} - \begin{bmatrix} X_1|O \\ X_2 \end{bmatrix} \tilde{\beta} \right\}' \left\{ \begin{bmatrix} y_1 \\ y_2 \end{bmatrix} - \begin{bmatrix} X_1|O \\ X_2 \end{bmatrix} \tilde{\beta} \right\}$$

$$= (y_1 - X_1\tilde{\beta}^*)'(y_1 - X_1\tilde{\beta}^*) + (y_2 - X_2\tilde{\beta})'(y_2 - X_2\tilde{\beta}).$$

But[3]

$$(y_1 - X_1\tilde{\beta}^*)'(y_1 - X_1\tilde{\beta}^*) = (y_1 - X_1\tilde{\beta}_1)'(y_1 - X_1\tilde{\beta}_1) + (\tilde{\beta}_1 - \tilde{\beta}^*)'X_1'X_1(\tilde{\beta}_1 - \tilde{\beta}^*)$$

and

$$(y_2 - X_2\tilde{\beta})'(y_2 - X_2\tilde{\beta}) = (y_2 - X_2\tilde{\beta}_2)'(y_2 - X_2\tilde{\beta}_2) + (\tilde{\beta}_2 - \tilde{\beta})'X_2'X_2(\tilde{\beta}_2 - \tilde{\beta}).$$

Hence

$$(y - X\tilde{\beta})'(y - X\tilde{\beta}) = [(y_1 - X_1\tilde{\beta}_1)'(y_1 - X_1\tilde{\beta}_1) + (y_2 - X_2\tilde{\beta}_2)'(y_2 - X_2\tilde{\beta}_2)]$$
$$+ [(\tilde{\beta}_1 - \tilde{\beta}^*)'X_1'X_1(\tilde{\beta}_1 - \tilde{\beta}^*) + (\tilde{\beta}_2 - \tilde{\beta})'X_2'X_2(\tilde{\beta}_2 - \tilde{\beta})]$$

that is,

$$Q_1 = Q_2 + Q_3$$

say. The Q's are quadratic forms. The rank of Q_1 is, of course, $(m + n - k)$.[4] The rank of Q_2 is $(m + n - 2k + 1)$.[5] Finally, the rank of Q_3 is not greater than $(k - 1)$.[6] From these three pieces of information, and from the theorem concerning the rank of a sum of quadratic forms,[7] it follows that the rank of Q_3 must be $(k - 1)$. Thus the quadratic form Q_1 is the sum of two quadratic forms the ranks of which add to $(m + n - k)$, the rank of Q_1. It follows from Cochran's theorem[8] that Q_2 and Q_3 are independently distributed as $\sigma^2\chi^2_{(m+n-2k+1)}$ and $\sigma^2\chi^2_{(k-1)}$, respectively. Hence

$$\frac{Q_3}{Q_2}\left(\frac{m + n - 2k + 1}{k - 1}\right)$$

is distributed as F with $(k - 1)$ and $(m + n - 2k + 1)$ degrees of freedom. Note, finally, that, under H_a, Q_2 remains unchanged but Q_3 grows larger on the average. The upper tail of the F-distribution therefore provides a suitable test of H_0.

ANALYSIS OF VARIANCE FOR TESTING HOMOGENEITY

	D.F.	S.S.
Source of residual		
Separate regressions	$m + n - 2k + 1$	$(\mathbf{y}_1 - \mathbf{X}_1\tilde{\boldsymbol{\beta}}_1)'(\mathbf{y}_1 - \mathbf{X}_1\tilde{\boldsymbol{\beta}}_1) + (\mathbf{y}_2 - \mathbf{X}_2\tilde{\boldsymbol{\beta}}_2)'(\mathbf{y}_2 - \mathbf{X}_2\tilde{\boldsymbol{\beta}}_2)$
Deviation from H_0	$k - 1$	
Single regression	$m + n - k$	$(\mathbf{y} - \mathbf{X}\tilde{\boldsymbol{\beta}})'(\mathbf{y} - \mathbf{X}\tilde{\boldsymbol{\beta}})$

A BIBLIOGRAPHY OF STUDIES OF THE DEMAND
FOR CANADIAN IMPORTS

ESTIMATES OF THE PARAMETERS of Canadian import demand are scattered through the literature and in unpublished theses and manuscripts. A select bibliography is assembled below. A detailed comparison of results would consume a great deal of space and be only mildly rewarding. For no two economists specify the import demand functions in the same way, no two use the same data, and no two employ the same estimating procedure.

One or two general comments on the bibliography are in order. The most striking feature of the existing published estimates is that in not a single instance has a statistically significant price coefficient been obtained. The failure may be partly illusory, the product of the employment of an inappropriate price variable —for example, Cheng, and Polak too, I think, correct the published f.o.b. index simply by applying the average *ad valorem* rate of import duty. To the extent that the failure is not illusory, it must be attributed, in the light of our results, to the fact that, with a single exception, all investigators have been content to deal with aggregate commodity imports. And Cheng, the exception to the rule, chose to work with categories whose components are extremely heterogeneous in end use and for which price series are not available.

Cheng has made separate estimates for the 'twenties and 'thirties on the ground that a break in structure occurred in the early 'thirties. Polak and Safarian, too, have detected a break. However, the break is, I think, a statistical illusion which results from the failure to employ a price variable.

BIBLIOGRAPHY

CHANG, TSE CHUN. *Cyclical Movements in the Balance of Payments.* Cambridge, 1951, p. 224.

CHENG, HANG SHENG. *Canada's Demand for Imports, 1926–1939.* M.A. thesis, George Washington University, 1953.

DE VEGH, IMRE. "Imports and Income in the United States and Canada," *Review of Economic Statistics,* XXIII (Aug., 1941), 130–46.

KLEIN, LAWRENCE R. *A Textbook of Econometrics.* White Plains, New York, 1953, p. 142.

POLAK, J. J. *An International Economic System.* London, 1954, p. 179.

RHOMBERG, RUDOLF R. "Canada's Foreign Exchange Market: A Quarterly Model," *International Monetary Fund Staff Papers,* VIII (April, 1960), 439–56.

SAFARIAN, A. E. *The Canadian Economy in the Great Depression.* Toronto, 1959, p. 104.

SLATER, DAVID W. *Canada's Imports.* Ottawa, 1957, p. 222. A study prepared for and published by the Royal Commission on Canada's Economic Prospects.

Dr. T. M. Brown, formerly of the Department of Trade and Commerce, Ottawa, and now at the Royal Military College, Kingston, Ontario, has since 1947 been experimenting with complete econometric models of the Canadian economy. Imbedded in each model is an aggregative import demand equation. Some of Dr. Brown's results will appear shortly in the *Canadian Journal of Economics and Political Science*.

NOTES

CHAPTER ONE

1. See David W. Slater, *Canada's Imports* (Ottawa, 1957), chapter II.
2. Guy H. Orcutt, "Measurement of Price Elasticities in International Trade, *The Review of Economics and Statistics*, XXXII (May, 1950), 125.
3. This point will be taken up again in chapter III.

CHAPTER TWO

1. David W. Slater, *Canada's Imports* (Ottawa, 1957).
2. The details of alternative classifications, and my reasons for preferring Slater's categories, are set out in appendix II.
3. Lists of the chief items assigned to each category can be found in Slater, *Canada's Imports*, pp. 177–80.
4. The fuels category is the sum of the coal and petroleum and petroleum products categories. In terms of the *Trade of Canada* code numbers, the reconciliation may be set out as follows:

  Coal = 7061 to 7069 *plus* 7075 to 7077

  Petroleum and petroleum products = 7141 to 7185

  Fuels = coal *plus* (petroleum and petroleum products) *plus* 7290 (gas for cooking) *plus* 9249 (electrical energy) *less* 7141 and 7143 (asphalt).

Whether, in value terms, fuels exceeds or falls short of the sum of coal and petroleum and petroleum products depends, therefore, on the relative magnitudes of, on the one hand, 7290 *plus* 9249 and, on the other hand, 7141 *plus* 7143.

5. A price series was constructed by this method for the chemicals category too. See appendix I.
6. Peter M. Mieszkowski ("Canadian Import Demand for Fuels: A Study of Aggregation Bias in Econometric Research," unpublished M.A. thesis, deposited in Redpath Library, McGill University, Montreal) has constructed indirect price series for petroleum and petroleum products, and for fuels. The series are, however, unreliable since in their construction several quite arbitrary assumptions concerning the costs of transportation had to be made.
7. The following is a brief chronological account of events. Britain abandoned the gold standard in September 1931. On September 29 (but retroactive to September 1) the official sterling rate was frozen at the old parity of $4.8667. On October 10 (but again retroactive to September 1) new "anti-dumping" laws were passed. The difference between the frozen official rate and another official rate, which was adjusted every fortnight in the light of movements in the free market rate, was paid as *extra* duty, over and above the "normal" assessments on the inflated official values. On October 23 the official rate was re-frozen at a new rate of $4.40 on those goods which entered (either free or dutiable) under preferential arrangements, that is, on the British content of imports billed in sterling. On March 22, 1933, the official rate was re-set at $4.25, again applying only to the British content of sterling imports. In the following month the market rate stabilized at $4.25 and this particular episode ended.

It must be added that there were also brief periods in the later 'thirties when the pegging of the official sterling rate resulted in the *under*valuation of sterling imports.

8. The official yen rate was pegged at 49.85 cents from December 1931 to August 1935.

9. See Jacques Parizeau, *The Terms of Trade of Canada (1869–1952)*, Ph.D. thesis (University of London, June, 1955). Parizeau's work is discussed further in n. 11 below and in chapter v.

10. In the case of petroleum and petroleum products, the DBS weights have been revised. Crude petroleum, which is given a weight of 0.34 in the DBS index, is given a weight of 0.76.

11. Alternatively, one or other of the published DBS import price indices might have been adopted (with whatever adjustments might be considered necessary). For the period 1913–39 an index of wholesale prices of imports was published. (For details of its construction, see DBS, *Prices and Price Indices* [1933]). The barrier to its use is an obvious one—it is available only for the inter-war period. On the other hand, for the entire period 1926–55 the DBS has published, in both Paasche and Laspeyres versions, what is essentially an f.o.b. index. (However, the index is based partly on Canadian wholesale, and even retail prices, of imports, and partly on United States wholesale prices. And manufactured goods are represented by a sub-index of the prices of constituent items and of hourly earnings in the United States manufacturing industry.) In 1948 it underwent a minor reweighting (in its Laspeyres version) and revision of the individual price series. Its coverage is approximately the same as that of the aggregative indirect price index employed in this study. The DBS series was not used for the very good reason that its correction for transport costs, import duties, and local Canadian taxes would have involved extra time and outlay, and, even after correction, it would have had no obvious point of superiority over the index actually used. For a highly competent critique of the published DBS price indices, see Parizeau, *The Terms of Trade of Canada (1869–1952)*, especially the appendix to chapter I. Parizeau has corrected the official series for the arbitrary customs valuations of 1931–33 referred to above, and for certain other biases, principally those stemming from the incorrect recording in certain years of the f.o.b. value of imports of Scotch whisky.

CHAPTER THREE

1. Guy H. Orcutt, "Measurement of Price Elasticities in International Trade," *The Review of Economics and Statistics*, XXXII (May, 1950), 117–32.

2. See also Ta-Chung Liu, "The Elasticity of U.S. Import Demand: A Theoretical and Empirical Reappraisal," *International Monetary Fund Staff Papers*, III (Feb., 1954), 416–41.

3. T. W. Anderson and Herman Rubin, "The Estimation of the Parameters of a Single Equation in a Complete System of Stochastic Equations," *Annals of Mathematical Statistics*, XX (March, 1949), 46–64.

4. See Trygve Haavelmo, "The Statistical Implications of a System of Simultaneous Equations," *Econometrica*, XI (Jan., 1943), 1–12; Orcutt, "Measurement of Price Elasticities in International Trade," 122–3.

5. Orcutt, "Measurement of Price Elasticities in International Trade," 123–5.

6. For the immediate postwar period, however, the rule may need some qualification, at least for those categories of imports of which the United Kingdom was the principal supplier. See also chapter IV, n. 8.

7. This has been proved for the case of normal variables by Haldane. See J. B. S. Haldane, "Moments of the Distributions of Powers and Products of Normal Variates," *Biometrika*, XXXII (April, 1942), 235.

8. Peter M. Mieszkowski has assembled some evidence that in the fuels group approximately constant returns prevail (*Canadian Import Demand for Fuels*).

9. $\text{Cov.}(P + \epsilon, \epsilon_1 - \alpha\epsilon) = \text{cov.}(\epsilon_1, P) + \text{cov.}(\epsilon_1, \epsilon) - \alpha[\text{cov.}(\epsilon, P) + \text{var.}(\epsilon)]$. The first term on the right-hand side is negligible by the argument of the preceding pages. The second term, which measures the covariation of the error with which P is measured and the error with which the relation is specified, may be assumed to be negligible also. Thus, since var.(ϵ) is necessarily positive, bias will be avoided only if the error of observation is negatively correlated, in appropriate degree, with P.

10. Orcutt, "Measurement of Price Elasticities in International Trade," 124–5, 129.

11. The outstanding exception to this generalization is the indirect price index for food and food materials.

12. See Carl Christ, "A Test of an Econometric Model of the United States, 1921–1947," National Bureau of Economic Research, *Conference on Business Cycles* (New York, 1951), 39, n. 9; and S. C. Tsiang, "Experimental Selection of Explanatory Variables and the Significance of Correlation" (abstract), *Econometrica*, XXIII (July, 1955), 330–1.

13. Special attention is often paid by econometricians to the forecasting ability of a model in "turning-point" years. This suggests that in addition to the usual tests of significance one might compare the residuals of years in which the dependent variable changed direction with the residuals of other years. I have never been able to understand why in forecasting tests greater weight should be accorded to turning-points; and I would not attach any significance to the differential "success" of my estimates at turning-points when success is measured by the size of the residuals. But I may have missed the point. In any case, the checks have been made. On the whole, the dependent variable was "explained" in the years of turnabout as well as in other years. For some categories—machinery and equipment, miscellaneous consumers' goods—the estimated equations perform less well at the turning-points than in other years; for other categories—food and food materials, and coal—they perform rather better. Some equations—those for food and food materials, coal—are more "reliable" in upturns than in downturns; others—those for furniture and household appliances, etc., miscellaneous consumers' goods, and petroleum and petroleum products—do better in the downturns.

14. This is perhaps an appropriate place to refer to a suggestion of Wold's, that more reliable estimates may be obtained of the coefficients of the remaining regressors if those regressors the coefficients of which differ insignificantly from zero are dropped. Wold's rule of thumb is plausible, however, only if the regressors are independent of each other, a condition which is not satisfied in the present instance. See H. Wold and L. Jureen, *Demand Analysis* (New York, 1953), p. 246.

15. See J. Durbin and G. S. Watson, "Testing for Serial Correlation in Least Squares Regression," *Biometrika*, 37 (Dec., 1950), 409–28, and 38 (June, 1951), 159–78; and J. Durbin, "Testing for Serial Correlation in Systems of Simultaneous Regression Equations," *Biometrika*, 44 (Dec., 1957), 370–7.

16. Minister of Finance, *First Annual Report on the Administration of the Emergency Exchange Conservation Act*, Schedule I (Ottawa, February, 1949) and *Second Annual Report on the Administration of the Emergency Exchange Conservation Act*, Schedule II (Ottawa, October, 1949). Minister of Trade and Commerce, *Report on the Administration of the Emergency Exchange Conservation Act*, Schedule III (Ottawa, February, 1949).

17. The procedure was suggested to me by Dr. T. M. Brown of the Royal Military College, Kingston, Ontario.

18. As a third alternative, available, however, only for aggregate imports, the base period equivalent of $300 million might have been added to the value of imports in 1948, the equivalent of $150 million to the value of imports in 1949. But this procedure begs the question of the effectiveness of the restrictions.

19. Violent in terms of time series which omit six war years. The year-by-year shifts might have been relatively mild.

20. J. J. Polak, Hang Sheng Cheng, and A. E. Safarian have suggested that a break in structure occurred in the early 'thirties. References to their work, and my reasons for rejecting the hypothesis, are set out in appendix VI.

CHAPTER FOUR

1. T. Gigantes, "The Market for Automobiles in Canada: An Econometric Study," unpublished M.A. thesis, deposited in Redpath Library, McGill University, Montreal.

2. The inclusion of the beginning stock may be justified by the following line of argument which, in its essentials, can be found in Richard M. Goodwin, "Secular and Cyclical Aspects of the Multiplier and the Accelerator," in *Income, Employment and Public Policy. Essays in Honor of Alvin Hansen* (New York, 1948), pp. 108–132, especially p. 120.

Suppose that the desired stock of automobiles, say S^*, is a linear function of disposable income, and the three prices, P_c'', P_i'' and P_h'': $S^* = \alpha + \beta Y + \gamma P_i'' + \delta P_h'' + \epsilon P_c$. But imagine that consumers adjust their actual stock S only with a lag, that, in particular, they attempt in any period to make up part only of the discrepancy between the desired and the beginning stock. Then the demand for automobiles during that period may be written as

$$D = k(S^* - S) + dS$$

where k is a positive constant, presumably less than unity, and d is the rate of depreciation of the existing stock. When substitution is made in this "adjustment equation" for S^*, it takes the form postulated in the text:

$$D = k\alpha + k\beta y + k\gamma P_i'' + k\delta P_h'' + k\epsilon P_c'' + (d - k)S.$$

Unfortunately, it is impossible to estimate separately β, γ, and δ (and the corresponding elasticities) unless an independent estimate of d (or k) is available. But, on *a priori* grounds, reasonable limits can be assigned to both d and k and, therefore, to *estimates* of β, γ, and δ. As a special case, $k = 1$, that is, consumers adjust their stock of automobiles without lag.

3. See appendix v.

4. The categories fuels and total imports are aggregates based on other categories.

5. The lack of postwar observations precluded the application of the F-test to automobiles, trucks, and parts.

6. Note, however, that in the case of beverages and tobacco the estimated price elasticity is positive for the interwar period and negative for the postwar years.

7. On the other hand, there does not appear to be any pattern of change in the income elasticities, at least for the five categories which appear to have undergone a break in structure. Gideon Rosenbluth has suggested that, in the postwar period, "import fluctuations were on the low side, in relation to those in output, in both absolute and relative terms." (G. Rosenbluth, "Changing Structural Factors in Canada's Cyclical Sensitivity, 1903–54," *Canadian Journal of Economics and Political Science*, XXIV (Feb., 1958), 40). Rosenbluth's conclusion was based on the study of quarterly data for the period 1946–54 and refers to the undeflated values of aggregate imports.

8. The following are three possible explanations of the break. Within each of the five categories a shift in demand away from the more price-elastic towards the less price-elastic commodities may have occurred. Or Harrod's "law of diminishing elasticity of demand" may have been at play (R. F. Harrod, *The Trade Cycle* [Oxford, 1936], pp. 21, 17–22, 86–7). Or, finally the *illusion* of a demand shift may have been created by the non-fulfilment of one or the other of the assumptions underlying the choice of estimating procedure. Such an illusion could derive from the conjunction of inherent non-linearities in demand and the differences between the prewar and postwar average values of the variables; or it could derive from the fact that, during the immediate postwar period, the elasticity of import supply was abnormally low, at least for those categories of imports of which the United Kingdom was the principal supplier. See above, chapter III, n. 6.

CHAPTER FIVE

1. I understand that some years ago work along these lines was initiated in the Economics Branch of the Department of Trade and Commerce in Ottawa; but the project was abandoned before it bore fruit.

2. It will suffice to sketch the evolution of the Canadian tariff during the post-Ottawa

'thirties. The Ottawa Agreements were negotiated during the summer of 1932. They provided for additional protection to United Kingdom suppliers against their competitors from the United States by (a) reducing the British preferential rate on a large number (81) of items; (b) by increasing the intermediate and/or general rates on as many (89) items; and (c) by reducing the British preferential rate *and* increasing the intermediate and/or general rates on a slightly smaller number (49) of items. The retreat from this preferential treatment of British goods began in 1935 with the signing of the Canada–United States Trade Agreement (which became effective on January 1, 1936). Most imports from the United States had entered under the general tariff schedule; they now came in under the intermediate (later, "most favoured nation") rates. Further, rates were lowered on machinery, some kinds of automobiles, fruit, and vegetables. In 1938 a second, less important agreement with the United States carried further the retreat from the Ottawa position.

3. Jacques Parizeau, *The Terms of Trade of Canada (1869–1952)*, Ph.D. thesis (University of London, June, 1955).

4. G. L. Reuber, "Anglo-Canadian Trade: Prices and the Terms of Trade, 1924–1954," *Review of Economics and Statistics*, XLI (May, 1959), 196–9.

APPENDIX I

1. T. Gigantes, "The Market for Automobiles in Canada: An Econometric Study," unpublished M.A. thesis, deposited in Redpath Library, McGill University, Montreal. See also David W. Slater, *Canada's Imports* (Ottawa, 1957), p. 73.

2. Sales and apparent consumption figures for the period 1925–55 are taken from Canadian Automobile Chamber of Commerce, *Facts and Figures of the Automotive Industry* (Toronto, 1959).

3. D.B.S., *The Motor Vehicle* (Ottawa, 1922–26).

APPENDIX III

1. In this phase of the work guidance was obtained from J. Harvey Perry, *Taxes, Tariffs, and Subsidies*, 2 vols. (Toronto, 1955), and from D. B. S. Memorandum 8502–504, *Principal Taxes and Rates: Federal, Provincial, and Selected Municipal Governments* (annual).

2. In June 1931 a 1 per cent excise tax was levied on nearly all imports. In the following year, the rate was raised to 3 per cent. In April 1934 the rate was reduced to $1\frac{1}{2}$ per cent in so far as it touched imports of British origin. In March 1935 British goods were exempted altogether. In 1939 the tax was abolished.

3. The rationale of the formula may be set out in the following way. Let f^r be the rail freight rate per unit of a particular commodity in the year under consideration, and let f^s be the ocean freight rate per unit of a particular commodity in the year considered. Further, let Σ_r indicate summation over all commodities imported by rail, and let Σ_s indicate summation over the set of commodities imported by sea. Then

$$F = \left(\sum_r x_0 f^r + \sum_s x_0 f^s \right) \Big/ \left(\sum_r x_0 f_0^r + \sum_s x_0 f_0^s \right)$$

$$= \left\{ \left(\sum_r x_0 f^r \right) \Big/ \left(\sum_r x_0 f_0^r \right) + \left[\left(\sum_s x_0 f_0^s \right) \Big/ \left(\sum_r x_0 f_0^r \right) \right] \right.$$

$$\left. \times \left[\left(\sum_s x_0 f^s \right) \Big/ \left(\sum_s x_0 f_0^s \right) \right] \right\} \div \left\{ 1 + \left(\sum_s x_0 f_0^s \right) \Big/ \left(\sum_r x_0 f_0^r \right) \right\}$$

$$= (F_r + \alpha_0 F_s)/(1 + \alpha_0).$$

4. The ocean freight bill was $19.9 million. See D.B.S., *The Canadian Balance of International Payments. A Study of Methods and Results* (Ottawa, 1939), p. 71.

5. United States Department of Commerce, *Business Statistics*, 1957 biennial edition, and the 1936 Supplement to *Survey of Current Business*.

6. Rail freight per ton was $1.80, lake freight per ton was $0.35. See D.B.S., *The Canadian Balance of International Payments*, pp. 75–6.

APPENDIX IV

1. It is assumed that P is a random variable. If P is an administered, that is, non-random variable, the notation $E(P)$ is, of course, inappropriate and should be replaced by the mean value notation, $\bar{P}$; but nothing of substance changes.

2. J. B. S. Haldane, "Moments of the Distributions of Powers and Products of Normal Variates," *Biometrika*, XXXII (April, 1942), 235.

3. Guy H. Orcutt, "Measurement of Price Elasticities in International Trade," *The Review of Economics and Statistics*, XXXII (May, 1950), 123–5.

APPENDIX V

1. The test proposed in this appendix differs in only minor respects from that formulated by C. Radhakrishna Rao in his *Advanced Statistical Methods in Biometric Research* (New York, 1952), pp. 112–14. Gregory C. Chow ("Tests of Equality between Sets of Coefficients in Two Linear Regressions," *Econometrica*, XXVIII [July, 1960], 591–605) and Richard E. Quandt ("The Estimation of the Parameters of a Linear Regression System Obeying Two Separate Regimes," *Journal of the American Statistical Association*, LIII [December, 1958], 873–80) may also be consulted. My notation and method of exposition follow that of Chow in most details. Quandt appears to have miscalculated his degrees of freedom (p. 877)

2. Note that $\tilde{\beta}^*$ is not the $(k-1)$-vector of least squares estimates of the coefficients in a regression involving $(k-1)$ independent variables. It is obtained from the k-vector of estimates of the coefficients in a regression involving k independent variables by omitting the kth element.

3. *Proof.*

$$(\mathbf{y}_1 - \mathbf{X}_1\tilde{\beta}^*)'(\mathbf{y}_1 - \mathbf{X}_1\tilde{\beta}^*) = [\mathbf{y}_1 - \mathbf{X}_1\tilde{\beta}_1 - \mathbf{X}_1(\tilde{\beta}^* - \tilde{\beta}_1)]'[\mathbf{y}_1 - \mathbf{X}_1\tilde{\beta}_1$$
$$-\mathbf{X}_1(\tilde{\beta}^* - \tilde{\beta}_1)]$$
$$= (\mathbf{y}_1 - \mathbf{X}_1\tilde{\beta}_1)'(\mathbf{y}_1 - \mathbf{X}_1\tilde{\beta}_1) + (\tilde{\beta}_1 - \tilde{\beta}^*)'\mathbf{X}_1\mathbf{X}_1(\tilde{\beta}_1 - \tilde{\beta}^*)$$
$$- 2(\tilde{\beta}^* - \tilde{\beta}_1)'\mathbf{X}_1'(\mathbf{y}_1 - \mathbf{X}_1\tilde{\beta}_1).$$

But, from (V.1b), the last term is zero.

4. The $(m+n)$ terms $(\mathbf{y} - \mathbf{X}\tilde{\beta})$ are connected by the k linear relations of (V.1a).

5. By reasoning similar to that of n. 4, the rank of $(\mathbf{y}_1 - \mathbf{X}_1\tilde{\beta}_1)'(\mathbf{y}_1 - \mathbf{X}_1\tilde{\beta}_1)$ is $(m - k + 1)$ and the rank of $(\mathbf{y}_2 - \mathbf{X}_2\tilde{\beta}_2)'(\mathbf{y}_2 - \mathbf{X}_2\tilde{\beta}_2)$ is $(n - k)$. Since the two sets of residuals are independent, the rank of Q_2 is equal to the sum of the ranks of these parts, $(m + n - 2k + 1)$ (see n. 7).

6. From (V.1a), $(\mathbf{X}'\mathbf{X})\tilde{\beta} = \mathbf{X}'\mathbf{y}$, that is,

$$\begin{bmatrix} \mathbf{X}_1' & \mathbf{X}_2' \\ \mathbf{O} & \end{bmatrix}\begin{bmatrix} \mathbf{X}_1|\mathbf{O} \\ \mathbf{X}_2 \end{bmatrix}\tilde{\beta} = \begin{bmatrix} \mathbf{X}_1' & \mathbf{X}_2' \\ \mathbf{O} & \end{bmatrix}\begin{bmatrix} \mathbf{y}_1 \\ \mathbf{y}_2 \end{bmatrix}.$$

Hence

$$\left\{\left[\frac{X_1'X_1|O}{O\ |O}\right] + X_2'X_2\right\}\tilde{\beta} = \left[\frac{X_1'}{O}\right]y_1 + X_2'y_2.$$

Taking into consideration (V.1b) and V.1c), this equation may be written as

$$\left[\frac{X_1'X_1}{O}\right][\tilde{\beta}* - \tilde{\beta}_1] = (X_2'X_2)(\tilde{\beta}_2 - \tilde{\beta}).$$

Hence, since $(X_2'X_2)$ is non-singular,

$$(\tilde{\beta}_2 - \tilde{\beta}) = (X_2'X_2)^{-1}\left[\frac{X_1'X_1}{O}\right]\tilde{\beta}* - \tilde{\beta}_1).$$

It follows that

$$Q_3 = (\tilde{\beta}_1 - \tilde{\beta}*)'X_1'X_1(\tilde{\beta}_1 - \tilde{\beta}*) + (\tilde{\beta}* - \tilde{\beta}_1)'[X_1'X_1|O](X_2'X_2)^{-1}\left[\frac{X_1'X_1}{O}\right](\tilde{\beta}* - \tilde{\beta}_1).$$

Thus Q_3 is a quadratic form in $(\tilde{\beta}_1 - \tilde{\beta}*)$ and, since $X_1'X_1$ is of rank $(k-1)$, the rank of Q_3 is at most $(k-1)$.

7. The rank of a sum of quadratic forms is at most equal to the sum of the ranks of the forms.

8. Harold Cramer, *Mathematical Methods of Statistics* (Princeton, 1946), p. 117.

INDEX

Lightning Source UK Ltd.
Milton Keynes UK
UKHW030613210722
406167UK00006B/667